Who Told You That You Were Naked?

A Study of the Conscience

Andrew Wommack

Unless otherwise indicated, all scripture quotations are from the *King James Version* of the Bible in the public domain.

Scripture quotations taken from the *Amplified Bible, Classic Edition* (AMPC), copyright © 1954, 1958, 1962, 1964, 1965, 1987 by The Lockman Foundation, All rights reserved. Used by permission.

Scripture quotations taken from *Young's Literal Translation* in the public domain.

Scripture quotations taken from the *New King James Version*. Copyright © 1982 by Thomas Nelson, Inc. Used by permission.

Who Told You That You Were Naked?
A Study of the Conscience
ISBN: 978-1-912351-31-2
© 2018 by Andrew Wommack Ministries Inc
P.O. Box 3333, Colorado Springs, CO 80934
www.awmi.net

Andrew Wommack Ministries - Europe
P.O. Box 4392,
Walsall, WS1 9AR, ENGLAND
awme.net

Andrew Wommack Ministries India
info@awmindia.net
www.awmindia.net

Also available in eBook from awmindia.net

Printed 2018

All rights reserved. No portion of this book may be reproduced, stored in a retrieval system, or transmitted in any form or by any means – electronic, mechanical, photocopy, recording, scanning, or other – except for brief quotations in critical reviews or articles, without the prior written permission of the publisher.

Contents

Introduction

Did you know that God is a good God and that He has a good plan for your life? In Jeremiah 29:11, God assures us, *"I know the thoughts that I think toward you . . . thoughts of peace and not of evil, to give you a future and a hope"* (*New King James Version*). Even though this is true, I believe that very few Christians walk in God's best for them and live the life of blessing and abundance that He has promised all of us. But why is this?

There may be a variety of reasons as to why a person is unable to receive God's promises, but I believe a major one has to do with the conscience. Have you ever wondered about your conscience? What is it exactly? Where did it come from? What purpose does it serve, and what role does it play in your life? Does it help you or hurt you?

In *Who Told You That You Were Naked?* I will answer all of these questions about the conscience and more. I'll also discuss how the conscience affects non-Christians and Christians differently and the effect it has on our relationship with the Lord. And I will explain the connection between the conscience and sin and what God has to say about sin in our lives. It's probably not what you think!

I'm convinced that the vast majority of Christians don't have a clue about how the conscience operates or the profound effect it has on their walk with God. If they did, they would no longer struggle with the fear, shame, guilt, and doubt that keep them from God's best.

The Bible has a lot to say about the conscience:

I exercise myself, to have always a conscience void to offence toward God, and toward men.

Acts 24:16

Now the Spirit speaketh expressly, that in the latter times some shall depart from the faith, giving heed to seducing spirits, and doctrines of devils; Speaking lies in hypocrisy; having their conscience seared with a hot iron.

1 Timothy 4:1-2

Holding faith, and a good conscience; which some having put away concerning faith have made shipwreck.

1 Timothy 1:19

Which shew the work of the law written in their hearts, their conscience also bearing witness.

Romans 2:15a

These are but a few of the many verses that give us insight into the workings of the conscience. It's important to understand these truths and learn how to apply God's Word to our everyday lives in this area so that we will no longer be spiritually hindered or defeated.

As you learn about your conscience through the teachings in this book, you'll also learn how to pray with boldness and confidence, how to receive God's promises for yourself and others, how to break free from fear and doubt once and for all, how to walk in a greater intimacy with Jesus, and much more.

Are you ready for God's best? Then let's get started!

CHAPTER 1

In the Beginning Was ...Death

Not too long ago, I was on an airplane, traveling to minister. I had fallen asleep, and the Lord woke me up with a startling question: "Who told you that you were naked?" Well, that certainly got my attention! I'll show you where God was going with that question a little later, but first let's look at the foundation scripture for what He wanted to share with me.

> *And the* L*ORD* *God commanded the man, saying, Of every tree of the garden thou mayest freely eat: But of the tree of the knowledge of good and evil, thou shalt not eat of it: for in the day that thou eatest thereof thou shalt surely die.*
>
> Genesis 2:16-17

In verse 17, the word *die* is the Hebrew word *mûwth*. This word was translated as *die* more than 400 times in the Old Testament. But here, God emphasized it and said "[you shall] *surely die*" (brackets added). In the Hebrew text, the word for *die* actually appears twice. It actually is saying, "[you shall] *die die.*" *Young's Literal Translation* states it like this: *"dying thou dost die."*

When Adam and Eve ate the fruit, they didn't die physically at that moment. In fact, Genesis 5:5 reveals that Adam lived to be 930 years old! Instead of dying physically right away, they died spiritually the instant they ate the fruit. Their physical death was a result of the spiritual death that came upon them inside.

This is a huge statement I'm making here that most people don't understand. Most people look at things from only a physical, natural standpoint, and they can't figure out why they're experiencing death in their lives. Death is not just physical. Things such as depression, fear, discouragement, and shame all stem from spiritual death. The wages of sin is death (Rom. 6:23). Therefore, anything that is a result of sin is a form of death.

When Adam and Eve ate the fruit, the very first thing that happened was that they realized they were naked. Then they became ashamed, and then they hid themselves from the Lord.

> *And the eyes of them both were opened, and they knew that they were naked; and they sewed fig leaves together, and made themselves aprons. And they heard the voice of the LORD God walking in the garden in the cool of the day: and Adam and his wife hid themselves from the presence of the LORD God amongst the trees of the garden.*
>
> Genesis 3:7-8

Fear and shame are results of spiritual death. We use a narrow interpretation or definition of dying when we talk about just physically losing our lives. Dying is much more than that. If we are living in shame, if we have insecurities in our lives, if we are fearful, that's part of death. The problem is spiritual separation from God, and these things are just the physical results of that.

Death Equals Separation

That word *die* in the Bible does not literally mean ceasing to exist the way most of us think of it. We think that when a person dies, it's all over, but that's not true. The Bible teaches that physical death is the separation of the soul and the spirit from the body, but we continue to live.

Here are just two of the many scriptures that talk about this:

> *And I saw thrones, and they sat upon them, and judgment was given unto them: and I saw the souls of them that were beheaded for the witness of Jesus, and for the word of God, and which had not worshipped the beast, neither his image, neither had received his mark upon their foreheads, or in their hands; and they lived and reigned with Christ a thousand years.*
>
> Revelation 20:4

> *For as the body without the spirit is dead, so faith without works is dead also.*
>
> James 2:26

When we put these verses together, we see that it's the spirit and soul that leave the body at death, and then the body collapses and returns to dust. In the Bible, death simply means separation. It never means ceasing to exist; no one ceases to exist. No one's life just "ends." A person's life does not end when his or her physical body dies. The person continues to live; it's just a matter of *where* that person will live.

There are only two possible outcomes as to where people will continue to live after their bodies separate from their souls and spirits. There's not a purgatory, or a third place, the way some believe.

Believers will go into the presence of the Lord.

> *To be absent from the body . . .* [is] *to be present with the Lord.*
>
> **2 Corinthians 5:8, brackets added**

Those who have not accepted the Lord will live a life separated from God for all of eternity:

> *And whosoever was not found written in the book of life was cast into the lake of fire.*
>
> **Revelation 20:15**

Those are the only two options, even though today's culture has drifted so far away from scriptural principles and a biblical way of thinking that we hear a lot of myths about eternity. For instance, when people die who have lived a life of total rebellion toward God and never cared anything about Him, some will say, "Well, at least they're at rest." They aren't at rest! Their lives just got worse—a lot worse.

That is just wrong thinking. The idea that when someone dies that means it's all over is certainly not what the Bible teaches. When Genesis 2:17 says that Adam and Eve would "surely die" the day they ate the fruit, it's saying that they would instantly be separated from God.

That's what death is. Sickness, emotional problems, financial problems, worry, fear, shame, and insecurities are all the physical results of being separated from God. I know that's a big statement. If it's true—which I will prove to you that it is—then the problem is that we've only been treating the symptoms and trying to deal with the external things.

There are coping mechanisms and ways of handling the symptoms, but the root of the problem is that we are living a life separated from God's love. The cure is to once again establish our relationship with Him and to build back the unity and love with Him we once had. When we do that, we will be set free from all the symptoms.

The Power of Doubt

> *Now the serpent was more subtil than any beast of the field which the LORD God had made. And he said unto the woman, Yea, hath God said, Ye shall not eat of every tree of the garden?*
>
> Genesis 3:1

It's interesting that Satan didn't choose an animal that would overpower or intimidate Adam and Eve. He didn't choose a lion or bear, for instance, which could threaten to kill them. Instead, he chose a subtle animal. He had to do this because he had no real power to force them to do anything. His only weapon was (and is) deception, and he had to get them to doubt God's Word.

He started by asking Eve, "Has God really said . . . ?" Satan had no power over them; he had to get them to initiate their disobedience, and he did so by challenging the Word of God. If we never doubted God's Word, we would never enter into sin. All of our problems come because, at some point or another, we believe the Enemy's lie. When we buy into a lie, we empower Satan in our lives.

If our values were based solely on the Word of God, we would never deviate from it. Satan would not be able to get to us. 1 Peter 5:8 warns:

> *Be sober, be vigilant; because your adversary the devil, as a roaring lion, walketh about, seeking whom he may devour.*

This verse proves that Satan can't devour everyone. If it were up to him, he would be killing all of us—physically, emotionally, financially, and every other way—but he can't do it. It's not up to him. Satan can't do anything to us without our consent and cooperation. He has to have our cooperation, even though we may not know we're cooperating with him.

There was a time when I was fearful of the opinions that people had of me prospering. I didn't realize that this was a problem I had, so I was unknowingly cooperating with the devil. I wasn't free to speak forth all of the things that God had shown me, because of my fear of what people might say.

It may not be sinful or malicious on our part, but, regardless, if Satan is destroying our lives, he had to have our cooperation to do so. Not many people like to hear this because they'd rather just blame other people for their problems. But just like with Adam and Eve, at some point, Satan has to get people to doubt God and turn on Him. He can't force people to do anything.

(I have an entire series called *Christian Philosophy* that goes into greater detail on this subject. I teach about six hours on what I'm touching on only briefly here. There is much, much more to this, so I encourage you to get this teaching for a more in-depth study on this matter.)

The Blame Game

The bottom line is that we need to quit blaming God or fate or other people for our actions. Some people think that it's everybody else, it's the way they're being treated, or it's "this woman You gave me!" That's exactly what Adam did. He passed the buck to Eve, and then he actually tried to blame God, saying, "God, You're the one who gave her to me!" He refused to accept responsibility.

> *And the man said, The woman whom thou gavest to be with me, she gave me of the tree, and I did eat.*
>
> Genesis 3:12

The first step to becoming free is to quit blaming everybody else for what's going on in your life and accept responsibility. It's actually a blessing to discover that you're the one who's wrong, because if you're the problem, you can fix you. In fact, you are the only one you can fix. If I'm your problem, you can't fix me.

This is one of the major issues in our nation today. People say, "It's the color of my skin, and if everyone would treat me differently . . ." or "It's my lack of money, and if the government would just give me more money . . ." We try to make everybody else treat us a certain way. We're putting the problem on everyone and everything else when the truth is, it's us.

Satan cannot do anything to us without our consent and cooperation. If our lives are all messed up, it's not because of what somebody else has done. Other people might have been used by the devil to hurt us, but we still have a choice as to whether we become bitter or better. The moment we say, "You don't understand. I was abused. I had this happen to me, and I had no choice," we violate the Word of God. First Corinthians 10:13 tells us:

> *There hath no temptation taken you but such as is common to man: but God is faithful, who will not suffer you to be tempted above that ye are able; but will with the temptation also make a way to escape, that ye may be able to bear it.*

This verse clearly says that we can choose the good instead of the bad. If it weren't that way, people who have been through the same traumatic experiences would have the exact same results in their lives because of the trauma. Yet this can be proven not to be the case. There can be two siblings with the exact same gene pool who were brought up in the same house and in the same environment, but one will go this way, and the other will go that way. One will become an alcoholic because the parents were alcoholic, while the other one will become a teetotaler and go in the opposite direction.

It's wrong to blame your environment and blame everybody else for the way you are. Other people may be a factor, but you still have a choice as to how you will respond. You were created in the image of God (Gen. 1:27), and you have a choice about whether you become bitter or better.

CHAPTER 2

Two Sets of Eyes

After Satan approached Eve in Genesis 3:1 and asked her, "Has God really said?" she responded to him in the next two verses:

> *And the woman said unto the serpent, We may eat of the fruit of the trees of the garden: But of the fruit of the tree which is in the midst of the garden, God hath said, Ye shall not eat of it, neither shall ye touch it, lest ye die.*
>
> Genesis 3:2-3

There are a couple of things wrong with Eve's response. First, the Lord didn't say that they couldn't touch the tree; Eve added that part. Second, she said that God had said *"lest ye die."* What He actually said was "surely" you'll die (Gen. 2:17). He emphasized that part; it was absolute, no question about it. But when Eve responded to Satan in Genesis 3:3, saying, *"lest ye die,"* it meant that "maybe we'll die," or "we might possibly die." It wasn't a definite.

You can't add to or take away from what God has said. You need to stick with exactly what He has said. If Satan can't get you to totally disagree with the Word, he'll get you to add to it or subtract from it. I have some friends who, by God's grace, have been set free from legalism and performance-based condemnation. But they have become so free that they've taken certain truths from the Bible and have chosen to disregard other truths. They now believe that there is no hell and no accountability to God.

I've countered some of them on it, and they've said, "Well, we just don't believe those parts of Scripture. We believe that those things don't apply to us today." That is exactly what Satan got Eve to do—to doubt and question the Word of God. It's dangerous to pick and choose which parts of the Bible you want to believe.

If you just say, "I'm going to believe this part, but I won't believe that part," what you're doing is making an idol. That's what an idol is. It's a god of someone's own creation. If people don't like God the way He is revealed in Scripture, they make their own carving and ascribe to it whatever traits and qualities they want, and they become idolaters. Most of us wouldn't create an image to worship, but when we pick and choose which parts of the Bible we want to believe, we're in idolatry. That's making our own god. We have to just take the Word of God and accept the revelation that has been given.

In Genesis 3:2-3, Eve added to and weakened what God said. At first, Satan just planted a question: "Has God really said?" The devil will never make a frontal attack on the things of God until he's planted a doubt. And here, he did just that. If we would deal with the doubt by saying "Yes, God has said . . ." and not entertain any thoughts that contradict God's Word, we could stop Satan right there.

Satan didn't start off saying to Eve, "No, God didn't say this; it's not true." He just planted a little seed and then made a bold-faced statement saying that what God said was not true:

> ***And the serpent said unto the woman, Ye shall not surely die: For God doth know that in the day ye eat thereof, then your eyes shall be opened, and ye shall be as gods, knowing good and evil.***
>
> Genesis 3:4-5

This is how Satan deals with us too. He doesn't start off saying, "You aren't healed." He will plant a doubt first. He'll say, "How do you know you are healed? Have you had it confirmed? What about so-and-so, who said they were healed and then died?" Only after doubt is present will Satan come directly against God's Word with the statement, "It didn't work. You aren't healed."

Our Sixth Sense

In Matthew 4:1-11, we learn that Jesus had three temptations come against Him.

> *Then was Jesus led up of the Spirit into the wilderness to be tempted of the devil. And when he had fasted forty days and forty nights, he was afterward an hungred. And when the tempter came to him, he said, If thou be the Son of God, command that these stones be made bread. But he answered and said, It is written, Man shall not live by bread alone, but by every word that proceedeth out of the mouth of God. Then the devil taketh him up into the holy city, and setteth him on a pinnacle of the temple, And saith unto him, If thou be the Son of God, cast thyself down: for it is written, He shall give his angels charge concerning thee: and in their hands they shall bear thee up, lest at any time thou dash thy foot against a stone. Jesus said unto him, It is written again, Thou shalt not tempt the Lord thy God. Again, the devil taketh him up into an exceeding high mountain, and sheweth him all the kingdoms of the world, and the glory of them; And saith unto him, All these things will I give thee, if thou wilt fall down and worship me. Then saith Jesus unto him, Get thee hence, Satan: for it is written, Thou shalt worship the Lord thy God, and him only shalt thou serve. Then the devil leaveth him, and, behold, angels came and ministered unto him.*

Hebrews 4:15 tells us that He was *"in all points tempted like as we are, yet without sin."* Jesus wasn't tempted with things like getting angry or frustrated with traffic or some of the other modern-day temptations that we have, yet He was tempted *"in all points . . . as we are."* This is because, according to 1 John 2:16, there are only three areas of sin (the three temptations that Jesus experienced in Matthew 4:1-11): the lust of the flesh, the lust of the eyes, and the pride of life.

> *For all that is in the world, the lust of the flesh, and the lust of the eyes, and the pride of life, is not of the Father, but is of the world.*
>
> 1 John 2:16

Continuing in Genesis, we see that Eve was confronted with these same three temptations:

> *And when the woman saw that the tree was good for food, and that it was pleasant to the eyes, and a tree to be desired to make one wise, she took of the fruit thereof, and did eat, and gave also unto her husband with her; and he did eat.*
>
> Genesis 3:6

But instead of resisting the temptations, she acted on them. Verse 7 tells us what happened when she and Adam ate the fruit:

> *And the eyes of them both were opened, and they knew that they were naked; and they sewed fig leaves together, and made themselves aprons.*
>
> Genesis 3:7

What does it mean that *"the eyes of them both were opened"*? Had their eyes been shut prior to this? This isn't saying that until that point, they had been walking around with their eyes closed. This scripture is talking about faith. God did not create mankind with just five senses the way most of us know it to be. He created us with six senses. That sixth sense is faith, and up until verse 7, Adam and Eve had been walking by faith. They had been seeing things with their hearts. However, sinning caused the eyes of their human understanding to open—and the eyes of their spiritual understanding to close.

We can see another instance of "eyes of spiritual understanding" in 2 Kings 6:15-17.

> *And when the servant of the man of God was risen early, and gone forth, behold, an host compassed the city both with horses and chariots. And his servant said unto him, Alas, my master! how shall we do? And he answered, Fear not: for they that be with us are more than they that be with them. And Elisha prayed, and said, LORD, I pray thee, open his eyes, that he may see. And the LORD opened the eyes of the young man; and he saw: and, behold, the mountain was full of horses and chariots of fire round about Elisha.*

Elisha prayed that his servant's eyes would be opened. This doesn't mean that the servant had his eyes closed. The servant was looking at the Syrians surrounding them, and he asked Elisha, *"How shall we do?"* That's the Old English way of saying that he panicked. He was saying, "What are we going to do?"

Elisha prayed and told him, "There are more with us than there are with them. Lord, open up the young man's eyes." And the Lord opened his servant's eyes.

This isn't referring to his physical eyes but rather the eyes of his heart. When his eyes were opened, he saw into the spirit realm. There is a spiritual realm that is just as real—actually more real—than this physical world. The spiritual world created this physical world. The spiritual world is the parent force. It will exist long after this physical world is annihilated and God creates a new heaven and a new earth.

> *And I saw a new heaven and a new earth: for the first heaven and the first earth were passed away; and there was no more sea.*
>
> Revelation 21:1

The *Real* You

The spiritual realm is more real than this physical world, and there's not only a spiritual world outside of here, but there's also a spiritual realm on the inside of you. This spirit realm is the *real* you. You are a spirit who has a soul and lives in a body, but the spirit is the life-giving part of you. In Genesis 2:7, God created Adam by breathing into him the breath of life:

> *And the Lord God formed man of the dust of the ground, and breathed into his nostrils the breath of life; and man became a living soul.*

The Hebrew word translated *breath* here is the same word that's translated *spirit* elsewhere in the Old Testament. God literally blew a spirit into Adam, and that's what gave him life. The life-giving part of you is your spirit. James 2:26 says that *"as the body without the spirit is dead, so faith without works is dead also."*

Your body is just your earth suit. If you wanted to go out into space, because of the temperature and lack of oxygen, you couldn't exist without a spacesuit. If you want to exist in this earth, you have to have an earth suit. Your body is your earth suit, but when you lose your earth suit, you don't cease to exist; you just go into a different realm—the spirit realm. (My *Spirit, Soul & Body* materials offer an in-depth study on the relationship among the three parts that make up every human being and how these three parts affect our walk with the Lord.)

Prior to Genesis 3:6-7, when Adam and Eve's eyes were opened, they had been walking by faith. They were dominated more by the spiritual world than the physical, and spiritual things had been more real to them. But when they ate the fruit, their spiritual eyes closed, and their physical eyes became dominant.

We think that the way we see, think, and feel right now is normal, but it's actually abnormal to the way God created us to be. Through the new birth, we have a new spirit on the inside of us. Paul said in 2 Corinthians 5:7 that *"we walk by faith, not by sight."* As New Testament believers, we should be the way that Adam and Eve originally were, where the spirit realm is more real to us than the physical, tangible realm. Yet I am sad to say that very few Christians live in the spirit realm. Instead, we live as physical, carnal beings who are controlled and dominated by what we see, taste, hear, smell, and feel.

In 2 Kings 6:15-17, Elisha's servant's normal condition was that his spiritual eyes were closed. Elisha prayed that his servant's spiritual eyes would be opened. That was the exact opposite of what happened with Adam and Eve. Adam and Eve had been walking by faith until they ate from the tree and their spiritual eyes closed. They stopped using their sixth sense, and instead their physical eyes were opened and were dominant.

Let's continue on in Genesis 3:

> *And they heard the voice of the LORD God walking in the garden in the cool of the day: and Adam and his wife hid themselves from the presence of the LORD God amongst the trees of the garden. And the LORD God called unto Adam, and said unto him, Where art thou? And he said, I heard thy voice in the garden, and I was afraid, because I was naked; and I hid myself. And he said, Who told thee that thou wast naked? Hast thou eaten of the tree, whereof I commanded thee that thou shouldest not eat?*
>
> Genesis 3:8-11

I began this book talking about how God woke me up on an airplane with a question. I now want to go back to that question. He woke me up with the same question He asked Adam in

Genesis 3:11: "Who told you that you were naked?" Think about that for a moment. Who told you that you were naked? This isn't talking about not wearing clothes. But who told you that you were defeated? Who told you that you were sick, depressed, discouraged, fearful, and all these other things that come as a result of sin? Where did you get this knowledge? Who told you all these things? Let's find out.

CHAPTER 3

The Tree

Some think that Satan was the one who told Adam and Eve they were naked, but there is no scriptural evidence for that. Other people believe that God told them, but Genesis 3:11 says, *"And* [God] *said, Who told thee that thou wast naked?"* (brackets added).

God didn't tell Adam and Eve that they were naked, so where did they get this information? How did they know they were naked? How did they know to hide from God?

> *And the LORD God called unto Adam, and said unto him, Where art thou? And he said, I heard thy voice in the garden, and I was afraid, because I was naked; and I hid myself.*
>
> Genesis 3:9-10

The Lord had never given them a reason to be afraid of Him. He had created the perfect environment, the perfect world. Everything was awesome! He had never rejected them. There was reason for them to have reverence for God, but not to fear Him. Adam and Eve had never done anything bad. Nothing in their existence had any rejection or punishment associated with it. So, where did they get this knowledge from?

God's question to Adam and Eve gives us the answer:

> *Hast thou eaten of the tree, whereof I commanded thee that thou shouldest not eat?*
>
> **Genesis 3:11b**

When they ate of the Tree of the Knowledge of Good and Evil, they intuitively and automatically recognized their nakedness, their sin, and their failure. Immediately, fear and shame came upon them.

I've heard a lot of people teach that Adam and Eve were clothed in the glory of God and in robes of righteousness, implying that they weren't truly naked. It's okay to make an allegory out of it and spiritualize it, but the truth is that they were completely physically naked.

> *And they were both naked, the man and his wife, and were not ashamed.*
>
> **Genesis 2:25**

God knew they were naked, but He never mentioned it to them. He never wanted mankind to be aware of their nakedness.

The Beginning of the Conscience

God didn't create us with a conscience. The *American Heritage Dictionary* defines *conscience* as "an awareness of morality in regard to one's behavior; a sense of right and wrong that urges one to act morally." God didn't create us with an ability to judge ourselves and to constantly evaluate whether we're right or wrong. He created us in innocence. Adam and Eve were totally naked, and according to Genesis 2:25, they *"were not ashamed."*

Hebrews 4:13 says, *"Neither is there any creature that is not manifest in his sight: but all things are naked and opened unto the eyes of him with whom we have to do."* To think that, somehow or another, our clothes can hide our shame and nakedness from God is just crazy. God isn't limited. Superman has nothing on Him! God can see right through us.

So, where did Adam and Eve get the knowledge of their nakedness? It came from the Tree of the Knowledge of Good and Evil. The name of this tree is descriptive of the conscience. I believe that when Adam and Eve ate from the tree, they received their consciences. One of two things happened: either God created man with a conscience that was originally inactive but was activated when they ate from the tree, or the tree actually gave them a conscience.

I tend to believe that the Tree of the Knowledge of Good and Evil created a conscience in mankind. The reason I believe this is because of what the Bible says the Tree of Life had the power to impart.

> *And the LORD God said, Behold, the man is become as one of us, to know good and evil: and now, lest he put forth his hand, and take also of the tree of life, and eat, and live for ever: Therefore*

> *the LORD God sent him forth from the garden of Eden, to till the ground from whence he was taken.*
>
> **Genesis 3:22-23**

Eating from the Tree of Life would have caused Adam and Eve to live forever. The tree could have literally imparted something to them. If this is true of the Tree of Life, then I believe that the Tree of the Knowledge of Good and Evil could also impart something.

> *He that hath an ear, let him hear what the Spirit saith unto the churches; To him that overcometh will I give to eat of the tree of life, which is in the midst of the paradise of God.*
>
> **Revelation 2:7**

And Revelation 22:1-2 speaks of the new heaven and the new earth, along with a river of life and a tree of life on both sides of this river:

> *And he shewed me a pure river of water of life, clear as crystal, proceeding out of the throne of God and of the Lamb. In the midst of the street of it, and on either side of the river, was there the tree of life, which bare twelve manner of fruits, and yielded her fruit every month: and the leaves of the tree were for the healing of the nations.*

By partaking of these trees and eating their leaves, life is literally imparted. That's what's going to happen in eternity, but that's also the way the Tree of Life was in Genesis. If that's the case, then I believe that the Tree of the Knowledge of Good and Evil also imparted something to Adam and Eve. This is where mankind gained a conscience; God didn't create us with one.

The Problem with the Conscience

What is the fruit of now having a conscience? The very first fruit can be found in Genesis 3:7.

> *And the eyes of them both were opened, and they knew that they were naked; and they sewed fig leaves together, and made themselves aprons.*

Having a conscience made Adam and Eve self-conscious, and they began to focus their attention on themselves. They weren't one bit more naked after they sinned than they were before they sinned. Nothing in the natural changed; it was their perception or focus that changed. A conscience makes you focus on yourself. A conscience makes you self-aware. Adam and Eve had been naked before, but they didn't even notice it. They were so God-conscious that they hadn't noticed their own nakedness.

In 2 Corinthians 5:7, we're admonished to *"walk by faith, not by sight,"* but let me just add that if you get so God-conscious that you don't even notice whether you've got clothes on, have mercy on the rest of us who are still carnal, and wear your clothes!

Now, Adam and Eve didn't even know they were naked, but once they ate of the tree, they became self-aware. They became fixated on self, and shame came upon them. Before, they had no shame, but all of a sudden, their consciences brought shame and fear of punishment.

These are things God never wanted us to have. He never wanted us to be afraid. He didn't create us for rejection; He created us for fellowship. He didn't intend for us to have a conscience, but after Adam and Eve sinned, it became necessary.

God Had a Plan

You might be thinking that it would be nice just to somehow or another get rid of the conscience. But for someone who's lost, a conscience is necessary because it makes them aware of their sin and shows them the need for forgiveness. I personally believe that this is the reason the Lord had the Tree of the Knowledge of Good and Evil in the Garden. He had to give us a free choice to serve Him. Otherwise, we wouldn't be free moral agents. We would only love Him and serve Him because there was no other option. God didn't want robots.

He had to give us the option. I don't believe it's just an accident that the option was the Tree of the Knowledge of Good and Evil, because the moment Adam and Eve ate from it, they received a conscience. Even though the conscience brings negative effects like shame and fear, it also provides a positive function, which is to show us that we have sinned and that we need forgiveness. So, I believe God had a plan for us since the beginning.

Revelation 13:8 shows us that God knew we were going to rebel against Him:

> *And all that dwell upon the earth shall worship him, whose names are not written in the book of life of the Lamb slain from the foundation of the world.*

He knew that we would sin and that Jesus would become the Lamb slain from the foundation of the world. Long before He even created us, He had planned everything out, and Jesus had already accepted God's plan for Him to come and redeem us. That's awesome. We could have a *selah* moment right here and just stop to think about that.

If I could somehow imagine myself being God and I were going to create man—knowing that mankind would rebel against me and that there would be terrible things like the Holocaust, divorce, ungodliness, hatred, hurt, pain, and everything else that has entered the human race—I don't think I would have created man, not after I knew all the pain man would cause.

The only way I can understand why God still created mankind is that He saw you and me—those who would accept His payment for sin and who would become new creatures, being born again in His likeness—and He decided that we were worth all of the pain and suffering. That's just amazing.

What establishes the value of something is what someone is willing to pay for it. I think of those little baseball cards that I could get for a penny when I was a kid. Those things are virtually worthless, as far as the actual substance of them, but now they've become rare, and people will pay a million dollars for one of these baseball cards. That establishes the value of them.

You may look at yourself or at me or at others and think, *Well, we aren't worth much*. But the very fact that God Almighty was willing to send His Son to earth and have Him die for us puts a huge value on us. As we just read in Revelation 13:8, Jesus was slain from the foundation of the world.

God knew everything that was going to happen, and it was already in His heart and mind. I believe that's why He made the Tree of the Knowledge of Good and Evil and the forbidden fruit. This way, if man did violate God's instructions (which He knew we would), then man would receive a conscience. This conscience would then immediately start condemning us and showing us that we are sinners who desperately need a Savior.

CHAPTER 4

The Role of the Conscience

Every person on earth has a conscience. It's impossible for anyone to not have a conscience. Romans 1:18-20 bears this out:

> *For the wrath of God is revealed from heaven against all ungodliness and unrighteousness of men, who hold the truth in unrighteousness; Because that which may be known of God is manifest in them; for God hath shewed it unto them. For the invisible things of him from the creation of the world are clearly seen, being understood by the things that are made, even his eternal power and Godhead; so that they are without excuse.*

Notice that it's not manifest *to* us; it's manifest *in* us (verse 19). Verse 20 tells us that the invisible things of God are clearly seen, not vaguely seen. Again, this is contrary to what most people believe today, which is that some people don't have any conviction over sin and just think that everything is okay. People say that religion has imposed the knowledge of right and wrong upon people, and everything would be so much better if it weren't for "religious folks" telling people what to do and not to do.

But Romans 1:18-20 clearly states that God has put this knowledge inside each of us. He's revealed Himself against all unrighteousness and ungodliness of man, and this revelation is manifest in them. It's already inside us. The conscience is like a homing device constantly telling us that we're failing, and even though that's painful and none of us like it, it's necessary for us to receive salvation. To become born again, we first must become aware of our need for salvation.

This is one of the things that's wrong with society today. It tries to make everyone think that they're okay no matter what they do—whether it's homosexuality or any other sin. Society attempts to justify everything and make sinners feel good about themselves, but people need to know that they're sinners. Jesus died for sinners. A person can't get saved unless they are a sinner. We first have to acknowledge our sinfulness and be aware of our need for God before we will ever satisfy that need by turning to the Lord.

I've read that the great revivalists of previous centuries would spend the first month of their meetings preaching on the wrath of God. Jonathan Edwards, who, along with George Whitefield, is credited with starting the Great Awakening in America, had a famous sermon called "Sinners in the Hands of an Angry God."

It is reported that people would be so fearful of hell as he preached that they would hold on to the pews in front of them until their knuckles turned white. They would literally see themselves falling into hell. Then, after they saw their sin and the impending judgment, Edwards would start preaching on the grace of God and revival would break out. It's only when we see our need for the Lord's salvation that we truly appreciate His grace. That's why we have a conscience.

Three (False) Gods in One

Romans 1:18-20 says that God has revealed Himself from heaven and that even His eternal power and Godhead is known. That is speaking of the Trinity—Father, Son, and Holy Spirit. I took pictures in Vietnam of a temple that was five stories tall. It was actually three temples that were built so closely together that no one could squeeze between them. They were three separate buildings all built together. The temples had trees growing out of them because they had been abandoned for such a long time.

I asked about the history of the temples and learned that they predated Christianity in Vietnam by 500 years. Five hundred years before Christianity reached Vietnam, these temples were there, and they were built to a god who was three in one! Am I saying that the people were worshiping the true God? No, I believe that they perverted the Godhead, and the temples probably weren't for worship of our true God. Nonetheless, it shows that they had the concept of three gods in one.

I saw something similar when I went to Chichén Itzá in Mexico. There, the Mayans used to conduct horrific games in which they murdered people by cutting out their hearts and offered people as human sacrifices to a god. There was a stone carving of this god, which manifests in three parts.

Vietnam had the concept of a triune god, and so did Mexico. How did this happen? There's no way that people in Vietnam influenced people in Mexico thousands of years ago. It was written in their hearts. Everyone has an intuitive knowledge of God. Everyone knows that there's only one God and that they are not Him! People can pervert this by worshiping multiple gods, but that's not the way they started out. Romans 1:21-32 talks about how people can walk away from the truth and can get to where they become reprobate.

Deep Down, We All Know

Paul told us in 1 Timothy 4:1-2 that we can get to a point where our consciences do not work as they should:

> *Now the Spirit speaketh expressly, that in the latter times some shall depart from the faith, giving heed to seducing spirits, and doctrines of devils; Speaking lies in hypocrisy; having their conscience seared with a hot iron.*

But no one starts out that way. We all begin with a conscience that is sensitive, knowing there is a God, knowing that we have sinned, and knowing that we need God. The conscience—our knowledge of good and evil concerning our own actions—came to us through the Tree of the Knowledge of Good and Evil. God intended for our conscience to point us to our need for Him, yet people today completely discount this.

There was a guy in Vietnam who claimed to be an atheist. He would always say that he didn't believe in God. He was a Princeton graduate. He came into my Bible study and asked all kinds of tough questions that I didn't know how to answer. He made a fool out of me with his questions in front of the seven guys in this Bible study. He said, "There isn't any God. I'm leaving! Who will go with me?" And the whole Bible study walked out with him.

After they all left, I was humiliated. I prayed and asked the Lord for another chance to reach this guy. In just a few minutes, he walked back into the chapel and sat down. He said to me, "I want what you have." I was shocked! He had just made a fool out of me to the degree that all the men in my Bible study left with him, yet he wanted what I had. I asked him, "Why?"

He said, "I'm a Princeton graduate and I was able to make a fool out of you. I embarrassed you, humiliated you, and outtalked you, but you still believe. You've got something that I don't have. My whole life is based on an argument, and if somebody was to out-argue me, I'd kill myself. But you've got something that's far more than just an argument."

I led this atheist to the Lord. In his heart he knew there was a God, but he had been denying it for so long that he had hardened himself toward the voice of his conscience. That's a dangerous thing to do.

I once had an employee whose parents were atheists and raised him to be that way too. He heard me preach on this—that everyone has an intuitive knowledge of God—and he told me he respected me, but he wasn't sure that this was true. He said he grew up with no knowledge or conviction that there was a God. It wasn't until he was an adult that he came to believe in God.

I told him that according to Scripture, it's not possible to *not* have a conviction that God exists. He might have been so influenced by his parents that he suppressed that inner witness, but based on Romans 1:18-20, it was there.

He came back to me later and shared something the Lord had brought to his remembrance. When he was around ten years old, he had climbed up a hill to watch the Los Angeles sunset. As darkness descended, he saw the lights come on all over the city below. There were millions of them.

He was thinking about how much work it took to set up all those lights. Each light had to be installed by someone and had to have wires run to it. Setting up those lights took thousands of people and many years to accomplish.

Then he lifted his head to look at the stars, and the thought came to him, *If each of the lights in the city had to be placed there by someone, how could you believe that the millions of stars just happened?*

At that moment, the Lord was speaking to him through that intuitive knowledge that Paul described in Romans. But the tradition this man received from his parents made him reject those thoughts (Mark 7:13). Nevertheless, they were there.

We all have a conscience that is constantly witnessing to us about our need for God, but we have to yield to it. It can be resisted.

In Acts 24:16, the apostle Paul said, *"I exercise myself, to have always a conscience void of offence toward God, and toward men."* You have to exercise your conscience. There are consequences if you violate it.

Each time you violate your conscience, it's like getting a callus on your hand. A layer of skin begins to form, and if the process continues, your hand can get so calloused that after a while you can't feel anything. I used to play guitar six nights a week, leading praise and worship in my Bible studies. My fingers had become so hardened from playing that twelve-string guitar that when they tried to get a blood sample by pricking my finger, my finger bent the pin. The pin could not penetrate that callus!

That's the way your heart can become. Your conscience can get so hardened that after a while it's not functioning. But the truth is, deep down, everyone knows there's a God. During the Vietnam War, lots of people claimed to be atheists. But once the bombs started dropping and the bullets started flying, all of those atheists cried out to the God they didn't believe in. It's a mind game and a lie. Even someone who tells you they don't believe in God will cry out, "Oh, God!" if a gun is put to their head.

Condemnation Can Be a Good Thing!

Believe what the Word says, not what people tell you. Everyone has a conscience. The conscience is the part that condemns us. Romans 8:1 tells us that there is no condemnation for those who are in Christ Jesus. We have to exercise ourselves to get rid of the condemnation and use the Word of God to purge our consciences, but the conscience is the part that condemns us. However, the conscience still has a place, even in the life of a believer. We should be sensitive to our consciences and not hardened toward them.

Some of you are thinking, *I thought you were a grace preacher.* I am a grace preacher. I'm telling you that God loves you and that He's not condemning you. If you've made Jesus your Lord, then God loves you and has forgiven you, but you will be condemned if you aren't seeking the Lord. There are two ways to purge your conscience: One is through the blood of Jesus and the truth of God's Word; the other is to not violate your conscience. According to 1 Timothy 1:19, we can shipwreck our faith if we don't have a good conscience:

> *Holding faith, and a good conscience; which some having put away concerning faith have made shipwreck.*

You won't be successful in believing God if your heart is condemning you. You need to use the Word to purge your heart from an evil conscience and know that even though you're not the person you're supposed to be, God still loves you. Other times, you need to quit giving your conscience a reason to condemn you.

First John 3:21 states that if your heart doesn't condemn you, you can have confidence toward God. And Hebrews 10:35 says to *"cast not away . . . your confidence, which hath great recompence of reward."* Your conscience is the part that gives you confidence or condemnation.

This is one reason people don't see greater manifestations of the things of God. Their own hearts—their consciences—are condemning them because they continually violate what God tells them to do. You can't prosper if you do that.

Romans 2:15 describes the function of the conscience:

> *Which shew the work of the law written in their hearts, their conscience also bearing witness, and their thoughts the mean while accusing or else excusing one another.*

Your conscience either accuses you or excuses you; it either condemns you or gives you confidence. It can build you up or tear you down, depending on whether it's a good conscience or an evil conscience. It will either shipwreck your faith or help your faith obtain the promises of God. We all have to deal with our consciences.

The first fruit of Adam's and Eve's consciences was a change in their perception. They began to see things differently compared to before. They became self-conscious—looking at themselves—and they entered into shame and fear. Our fear and shame come from our consciences. To a large degree, the world recognizes this. They may not call it the conscience, but they're aware of condemnation. Psychology acknowledges guilt, shame, and unworthiness as the root of most problems. This is why people think it's important to have a positive self-image.

Sometimes It's Good to Feel Bad

Today, when children compete against each other, no one wins or loses because they're all supposed to feel good about themselves. My granddaughter received an award one day, and my son asked her why she had received it. She said everyone got one; there weren't

any winners or losers. My son threw the award away, saying, "That's wrong. Somebody won, and somebody lost. You need to realize that some people are better at certain things than you are."

I know there are people who think that this is the wrong way to deal with children, but we live in a fallen world. Everything isn't fair. There are winners and losers, and to just ignore these facts does not prepare children for what lies ahead. They need to learn that they will be rewarded when they perform well, and they will suffer consequences when they fail.

We've got this thing today where we don't want anyone to feel bad. That's wrong. The way we are supposed to make ourselves feel good isn't by making everyone else as bad as we are or by tearing others down. This is what a lot of people do. Instead of rising to your level, they'll just tear you down to where they no longer feel any conviction.

This is just Andyology, but I believe the reason that those who push the homosexual agenda are so intolerant of anyone who doesn't agree with them is that their consciences are condemning them. They don't purge their consciences through the Word and receive forgiveness. Rather, they try to make everyone else agree that their lifestyle is normal and acceptable. It's why they're so aggressive and militant. Their consciences are driving them, and they don't understand that the way to purge their consciences isn't to defile them and numb them or to compare themselves to other people. Instead, they should follow Hebrews 10:22:

> *Let us draw near with a true heart in full assurance of faith, having our hearts sprinkled from an evil conscience, and our bodies washed with pure water.*

They need to go to God, and the blood of Jesus will cleanse them and purge them of an evil conscience. It will take away all guilt and all shame. The way to get rid of shame isn't by trying to make everyone equal and saying that everything is okay and that it doesn't matter what you do. And it isn't by changing the rules and standards. The standards are there for a purpose. People need to feel guilty! They need to feel rotten when they sin.

It's similar to the way our bodies feel pain. No one likes pain, but it serves a purpose. If you place your hand on a hot stove, the pain you feel makes you remove your hand before you have time to think about it. It's just a reflex. Imagine what would happen if you couldn't feel pain when you touched something hot. You could burn your hand without knowing it and injure it to the point that it would be useless. Likewise, the conscience and the negative feelings it produces serve a purpose.

God didn't create us to have a conscience, but as a result of the Fall, everyone now has one. Its purpose is to let us know that we are a mess and need a Savior. But our society is doing everything it can to deaden people toward their consciences. Unfortunately, "religious" Christianity is doing the same thing. It won't say things are right and wrong; everyone's okay, no matter what people are doing. The truth is, if people are living in sin, they should feel bad, but they shouldn't continue to feel bad. They need to go to God to have their consciences purged and obtain forgiveness to become free from that guilt.

Grace doesn't change the fact that people are sinners. Grace loves sinners and extends mercy to them, even in the midst of their sin. My wife, Jamie, and I were talking with a friend whose son is a homosexual. This person loves their son. Parents of homosexuals love their children and don't want to reject them, but how do they continue to love them and yet not approve of their lifestyle? Nowadays, if you tell homosexuals they're in sin, they immediately fire back, "You hate me, and you're condemning me!" I'm not condemning them; it's their consciences that are condemning them. Disagreeing with what they're doing doesn't make me a hatemonger.

Speak the Truth in Love

Leviticus 19:17-18 says that if we love someone, we will tell that person the truth:

> *Thou shalt not hate thy brother in thine heart: thou shalt in any wise rebuke thy neighbour, and not suffer sin upon him. Thou shalt not avenge, nor bear any grudge against the children of thy people, but thou shalt love thy neighbour as thyself: I am the* Lord.

We can't say, "I'm not going to say anything because I don't want to be a hatemonger, and I don't want to condemn anyone." We can try to whitewash it anyway we want, but then we aren't telling people the truth. John 8:32 says that the truth sets people free. Love doesn't set people free; the truth does. The truth must be spoken in love (Eph. 4:15). We can't use the Bible like a club to beat people up and hurt them, but we must tell them the truth so they can be free. If we don't tell people the truth, Leviticus 19:17 says that we hate them. Many Christians would rather not say anything because they want to walk in love. But what they're doing is walking in love for themselves instead of other people. They don't want to suffer the persecution, the rejection, and the eye rolls from people.

One night, I was driving home on a steep, curvy mountain road. It was so foggy that I could only see several yards in front of me. I was going about fifty miles per hour on a four-lane divided highway, and a driver passed me like I was standing still. He got a little ways ahead of me and then slammed on his brakes, and his car jerked. It was obvious he hit something, so I slammed on my brakes and stopped right next to him.

I was on the shoulder, he was in the right lane, and in the left lane was a horse that he hit. The horse had landed on his windshield and caved it in. I went over to his car and saw him lying there bloody and badly injured. While I was standing there, a Suburban came around the corner going about sixty miles an hour. It hit the horse and launched itself more than five feet in the air and about twenty feet down the road. The driver was able to control the car once it hit the road again. I ran to the car and saw a dent in the roof where the driver's head may have hit.

I then ran back down the road and around the corner before anyone else could come upon the wreck. I started jumping out in front of cars that were going sixty miles an hour. They were nearly hitting me because visibility was so bad. Then I'd jump off the road, and they'd skid and slide. They were screaming at me, calling me every name in the book. But when they got around the corner and saw what was happening, they realized I was saving their lives. I bet all those people who cussed me out and waved at me with one finger were thanking me and blessing me as they came upon that wreck.

My point is, if you really loved people, you would take a risk like that. It was nearly thirty minutes before police came, and there must've been at least twenty cars that I flagged down. If you love people more than you love yourself, you'll be brave enough to tell them the truth—even if you might be hated for it. Sadly, in our society today, if you take a stand against sin, you'll be called a hatemonger, prejudiced, and biased. But what people say about you is not true; you are walking in love by telling the truth.

I once had a man ask me a question, and I knew he wasn't going to like the answer I had for him. As he was talking, I was thinking to myself, *Do I tell him the truth? He might get mad.* As I pondered this, the Lord spoke to me and said, "Don't reject the truth for him. He deserves the right to reject the truth for himself, if that is what he chooses to do." That changed me. I don't have the right not to tell people the truth. If I don't tell them the truth, it is just because I love myself more than I love them.

CHAPTER 5

Dangers of a Seared Conscience

When it comes to the issue of homosexuality, I don't care how many laws they pass or how many parades they have; I guarantee that homosexuals' consciences tell them they're wrong. They're miserable. The conscience cannot be purged apart from the blood of Christ (Heb. 9:14). But it can be numbed and seared. It can become reprobate.

> *And even as they did not like to retain God in their knowledge, God gave them over to a reprobate mind.*
>
> Romans 1:28

In other words, when people decide of their free will to refuse the knowledge of God, He surrenders them to a reprobate mind. At that point, He basically says, "If that is what you want, you can have it." Anyone who is surrendered to a reprobate mind no longer has a conscience. That's what makes them reprobate. Their conscience has been destroyed. And once that happens, they cannot be saved. They cannot return to the Lord. According to Romans 1, this is the last step away from God, and it is a terrible situation. You never want to get to a place where your conscience has been turned over to a reprobate mind. Many people will never get to this point, but there are others who have become so deadened to their conscience that it no longer functions.

In 1999, one of the deadliest school shootings in history took place at Columbine High School in Colorado. Afterward, there was a lot of talk about how we need to ban guns and take guns away from people. An elderly man wrote in to the Colorado Springs newspaper saying that when he was a kid, they had a one-room classroom, and every kid in the school had a gun and brought it to school. They used their guns to protect themselves from animals or whatever, but everyone brought a gun to school, and nobody ever got shot. He was making the point that guns aren't the problem. Guns don't kill people any more than forks make people fat.

A lot of this has to do with the fact that a generation ago, people believed in heaven and hell, and they were aware that although they may not have been living for God, there was a hell. They were afraid of standing before God one day and having to answer for their actions. It changed the way people behaved.

This is the point that Psalm 36:1 and Proverbs 16:6 make:

> *The transgression of the wicked saith within my heart, that there is no fear of God before his eyes.*
>
> **Psalm 36:1**

> *By mercy and truth iniquity is purged: and by the fear of the LORD men depart from evil.*
>
> Proverbs 16:6

In the Columbine shooting, the two kids who killed all of those people killed themselves afterward, thinking that they would escape prosecution. That's because they had no awareness of hell. They now know differently.

> *Speaking lies in hypocrisy; having their conscience seared with a hot iron.*
>
> 1 Timothy 4:2

According to this verse, our consciences can be seared. People don't understand that someday they're going to stand before God. Not having recognition of this dulls them to the voice of their consciences. This concept can be seen at work in nearly all mass shootings. The killers go into the situation expecting to get killed, or they kill themselves, thinking that they could literally get away with murder and escape the consequences through death.

But if they had consciences that were functioning according to the Word of God, they wouldn't do that. Just one generation ago, people behaved differently, not because human nature was different, but because people had consciences that put fear in them and made them afraid of doing certain things. Really, the conscience—or lack thereof—is where the problem lies. We can't put enough metal detectors in schools to stop all the trouble. But if there was prayer, if there were Bible studies, if the Gospel was taught, and if people were thinking about God and were aware that someday they would stand before Him and give an account of their actions, things would change.

Our society, however, is doing everything possible to kick God out of schools, to take the Ten Commandments out, and to take the knowledge of God away. The more removed from God we become, the less our consciences function the way they should. It's really a crisis of conscience that is the problem in this nation.

So, again, even though the conscience has negative effects like condemnation, guilt, shame, and fear, it's still necessary. Every person who has been born after Adam and Eve—every one of their descendants—was born with a conscience. According to Romans 2:15, God gave it to us to either accuse us or excuse us, to reveal our need for God, and to show us the things that are wrong in our hearts. The conscience is something that we have to deal with. It's a part of every single person's life.

A Defiled Conscience

It's important to remember that your conscience is not a perfect guide. As stated in 1 Timothy 4:2, the conscience can be seared. And, according to Titus 1:15 and 1 Corinthians 8:7-8, it can be defiled and weakened:

> *Unto the pure all things are pure: but unto them that are defiled and unbelieving is nothing pure; but even their mind and conscience is defiled.*
>
> Titus 1:15

> *Howbeit there is not in every man that knowledge: for some with conscience of the idol unto this hour eat it as a thing offered unto an idol; and their conscience being weak is defiled. But*

> ***meat commendeth us not to God: for neither, if we eat, are we the better; neither, if we eat not, are we the worse.***
>
> **1 Corinthians 8:7-8**

First Corinthians 8:7-8 talks about eating meat that's been sacrificed to idols. Paul was saying that there's really nothing wrong with the meat. An idol is nothing, so if you take meat that was sacrificed to an idol and want to eat it, there's no difference between that meat and any other meat, because an idol is nothing.

This was an issue with the first-century church, where a lot of people were idol worshipers. If people bought meat in the market that had been offered to idols, to them it was as if they were participating in idol worship. They thought that was terrible, yet some people understood the grace of God and said, "This really is no big deal. The meat isn't defiled. That idol is nothing, and therefore, it doesn't matter if I eat the meat that was offered to an idol." It was cheaper meat, and they got a good deal on it.

Because some thought it was okay to do this, Paul said to them in 1 Corinthians 8:1 that knowledge puffs up, but love edifies. He told them that they needed to walk in love with one another, and even though they might technically be correct and it might be okay for them to behave certain ways, they might be causing other people's consciences to be defiled. If people with weak consciences saw them eat the meat that had been sacrificed to idols, they would be emboldened to do the same. Yet in their minds, in their way of thinking, they would be participating in idolatry. So, by eating the meat, their weak consciences would be defiled (1 Cor. 8).

This same thing was spoken about in Romans 14:23, where Paul again talked about eating meat that was offered to idols:

> ***But the man who has doubts (misgivings, an uneasy conscience) about eating, and then eats [perhaps because of you], stands condemned [before God], because he is not true to his convictions and he does not act from faith. For whatever does not originate and proceed from faith is sin [whatever is done without a conviction of its approval by God is sinful].***
>
> **Romans 14:23,** *Amplified Bible, Classic Edition*

In the *King James Version*, this word *condemned* is actually rendered *damned.* But it isn't talking about people being damned in the sense that they lose their salvation but, rather, that they come under condemnation. Your conscience can make you guilty about things that there's nothing wrong with.

Always Condemned

I was raised in a very strict home. I would see a word of profanity scribbled on a bathroom stall, and it would condemn me. I didn't write it; I just saw it. But if that word even crossed my mind, I would beg God to forgive me for seeing it, even though I didn't have anything to do with it. I was also taught that we couldn't go "mixed bathing." Although it was just boys and girls in the same pool, they called it mixed bathing. That made it sound worse than mixed swimming! So, I wouldn't go swimming if there were girls present. I lived in constant condemnation.

When I was a kid, I had dreams for nearly ten years that I smoked a cigarette and got caught. I got turned in to the police, who turned me over to my mother, who "whupped" me, and then I wound up in hell. I'd wake up in a cold sweat because, in my dreams, I went to hell for smoking a cigarette. I've never smoked a cigarette in my life! Smoking a cigarette will not send you to hell. It will make you smell like you've been there, but it won't send you to hell. My dad smoked cigarettes, and he was the chairman of the deacons at our church. But someone told me that smoking was wrong, and it activated my conscience to where just the thought of smoking a cigarette sent me into a panic.

My conscience was really sensitive because of some things I was taught. I used to be condemned and feel terrible about things I shouldn't have felt bad about. In a way, that's bad, but in another way, it kept me from doing some things I probably shouldn't have been doing.

My, How Things Have Changed

Your conscience can change depending on your background and environment. One time, a guy was shoeing my horse and talking about how he and his girlfriend went to the same church as me. He wouldn't stop talking about this girl, so finally I asked him, "Are you married to this girl?" He said, "Oh, no. We just live together. We thought it would be helpful to kind of try it out. When you buy a car, you have to drive it around the block to see if you like it. We thought we'd decide whether we liked each other before we made a commitment and got married."

I just couldn't believe it. I asked, "Do you realize what the Bible says about this?" He asked, "What does it say?" So, I shared the Word with him. It usually takes thirty minutes to shoe a horse, but this time it took over three hours! He just soaked up everything I had to say, and finally said, "I didn't realize that. Well, we're going to get married." And they did. But nowadays we're taught that it's just wisdom to "shack up" with a person. Many people say, "Marriage is just a piece of paper; it doesn't mean anything."

In John 4:16-18, Jesus confronted a woman about her relationships:

> ***Jesus saith unto her, Go, call thy husband, and come hither. The woman answered and said, I have no husband. Jesus said unto her, Thou hast well said, I have no husband: For thou hast had five husbands; and he whom thou now hast is not thy husband: in that saidst thou truly.***

You know that this woman had had physical relationships with those husbands, yet Jesus said, "This one you have now is not a husband." "Shacking up" together is not marriage. There are reasons people don't commit themselves to another person in marriage, and none of them are good. My point is that a lot of people aren't influenced by God's Word but rather by the world. They have a world philosophy instead of a Christian philosophy. If you're taught this way, it dulls your conscience and keeps it from working properly.

I knew a man named Arthur Burt who died at 102 years old. He lived in Wales, and our Bible college took its very first overseas missions team to visit him. One time he came and ministered to our students, and I asked him about some of the differences that he'd seen in his lifetime, because at that time he was in his nineties. He said that when he was a kid in Wales, women had to wear swimming "costumes" (swimsuits) that were up to the neck and all the way down to the ankles and to the wrists. Every part of a woman's body was totally covered, except her hands, feet, and head.

In addition to that, the women had to go into a little room that was on wheels with a donkey attached to it to change into their swimming costumes. Then they would have the donkey take them out into the water, and the door would have to open away from the shore. Then they had to jump into the water really quickly. When they wanted to get out, they'd have to raise their hands, and the donkey would be brought back to the water so they could jump into the room again to change clothes.

That's the way it used to be. But now, bikinis are the norm, and some places even have nude beaches. If you were raised in an environment like Arthur's, your conscience would be very different from the conscience of someone being raised today. There are some people today who are told that being naked in public isn't even wrong. Where do people get their sense of conscience?

Cultural or Scriptural?

The first time I ever ministered in Austria, I was shocked. I was brought up in a Baptist church where if you smoked a cigarette, you were going to hell; if you took a drink of liquor, you were going to hell. At my meetings in Austria, there were about a hundred people who sat at round tables of ten. They were served beer—free beer—for as long as I wanted to talk. So, they all drank beer while I preached. It was one of the few times nobody cared how long I talked! It was hard on my Baptist brain to see these Christians drinking beer. You could drink beer there, but if you drank coffee, you would go straight to hell. You couldn't pass "Go," couldn't collect $200; you just went to hell if you drank coffee!

Another time, when I first started preaching in England, we took our kids with us. We'd go out to eat with the pastors, and they'd all drink beer and even offer my kids beer. I'd say, "No, you aren't having any beer." In Romania, Christians drank beer and coffee. But if you smoked a cigarette there, you were going to hell. I began to recognize that these things are more cultural than they are scriptural. I'm not saying that you should run out and drink. I've never taken a drink of liquor in my whole life, and I never plan on doing so. I'm not advocating it. But I'm saying that you won't go to hell for drinking wine with your meal.

In John 2:1-11, Jesus turned water into wine, and a lot of it! But again, consider 1 Corinthians 8, which I discussed earlier. There are a lot of people who, if they see you drinking alcohol, will be emboldened to drink also, and they might become addicted. Then you'd be participating in helping to destroy someone else. It's not wise.

When I pastored a church in Childress, Texas, Don Krow was my associate pastor. One day, he was cleaning out a carwash, and he found a six-pack of beer in the trash. He dug it out and put it in his refrigerator to use for beer-battered onion rings. I saw it in his refrigerator and told him, "It's not a problem to me, but we're going to have our church members coming over, and if they see a six-pack of beer in your fridge, it's not a good witness. You need to get rid of it."

You can see how your conscience can get skewed by the way you've been brought up, by things people have told you, or by the environment you live in. In the next chapters, we'll look at some other dangers that can produce a seared conscience.

CHAPTER 6

It's Only a Little "White" Lie

Now the Spirit speaketh expressly, that in the latter times some shall depart from the faith, giving heed to seducing spirits, and doctrines of devils; Speaking lies in hypocrisy; having their conscience seared with a hot iron.

1 Timothy 4:1-2

Here, Paul was speaking of the last days, which is the time we are living in right now. The phrase *"having their conscience seared with a hot iron"* can be compared to cauterizing a wound. This kills all feeling in that area. You can take something hot and use it to seal the wound. In the same fashion, you can do this with your conscience. You can sear your conscience as with

a hot iron. First Timothy 4:2 says it happens by *"speaking lies in hypocrisy."*

Let's just be honest about this. When you lie, it's not usually an out-and-out lie, but rather an exaggeration. Every time you misspeak, however, you are searing your conscience. Your conscience knows that what you're saying is not exactly right. In the Ten Commandments, God didn't say, "Thou shalt not lie." The commandment was *"Thou shalt not bear false witness"* (Ex. 20:16).

There are a lot of people who bear false witness constantly. They'll use statistics and polls and manipulate them to fit their needs. It may not be an outright lie, but it is false witness. I just heard a couple of weeks ago that during the recent midterm elections, conservatives across the board won some of the major elections, like this country has never seen. In Kentucky, a man was voted to be governor who ran as a Christian on a Christian platform, standing for morality and Christian values, and he beat his opponent two to one. The same thing happened in Houston.

There were some great victories for conservatives. Someone asked a prominent conservative radio host how, since all of the polls said it was going to be a landslide *against* conservatives, did so many conservatives win? He explained that when they poll, they take the number of registered Democrats versus the number of registered Republicans; then they consider other factors, such as whether Democrats might do better at getting people to vote and so forth, and they interpret the polls considering these influences.

If they take a survey and it's fifty-fifty on the way people say they'll vote, they'll take into consideration that there are more Democrats—giving more weight to the Democrats. Then they'll factor in that Democrats will get more people out to vote. They can take a fifty-fifty poll and make it two-to-one that Democrats will win because they weighted the polls. They claim it's a scientific survey, but it's false witness. It's not an accurate poll. Unfortunately, this has become common practice.

The other part of 1 Timothy 4:2 talks about hypocrisy. Hypocrisy is knowing that what you're saying or doing isn't right, yet putting on a façade. In fact, the word translated *hypocrisy* means "acting under a feigned part" (*Strong's Concordance*). The word originally was used to refer to actors hiding behind a mask. A hypocrite pretends to be someone or do something that is not genuine. Every time a person isn't genuine and says something in hypocrisy or misrepresents something, they sear their conscience with a hot iron.

Lying has become a totally accepted practice. It's so bad in politics that they've actually come up with a test to tell if politicians are lying. If you look at a politician square in the face and their lips start moving, they're lying! Of course, that's not true of all politicians. There are godly men and women in politics. But all too often, politicians will say whatever it takes to get elected; it's become the norm.

People are sick and tired of liars—people bearing false witness. Every time you lie, you sear your conscience with a hot iron, and it gets worse and worse.

Doctrines of Devils

Aside from bearing false witness, 1 Timothy 4:1-2 tell us that our consciences may also be seared when we give heed to *"doctrines of devils."* Verse 3 expounds on what these doctrines are:

> *Forbidding to marry, and commanding to abstain from meats, which God hath created to be received with thanksgiving of them which believe and know the truth.*
>
> 1 Timothy 4:3

Did you know that forbidding people to marry and preaching celibacy, such as saying that those in the priesthood have to be celibate, is a doctrine of devils? I'm not against anyone; I'm just reading Scripture. It's no coincidence that there's a rash of homosexuality and other sexual sin among priests who are forced into celibacy. It's because they're going against their natural order. In Genesis 2:18, God said, *"It is not good that the man should be alone; I will make him an help meet for him."* There are some cases where a person may be called to remain single, but that's the exception rather than the rule. According to 1 Timothy 4:1-3, it's a doctrine of the devil for you to tell a priest that he should be celibate. A person who does sears their conscience.

First Timothy 4:3 also talks about abstaining from meats. Many Christians today, under the guise of preaching healthy eating, will tell you that you shouldn't eat certain meats. But this verse says that is a doctrine of the devil. Verses 4-5 go on to say:

> *For every creature of God is good, and nothing to be refused, if it be received with thanksgiving: For it is sanctified by the word of God and prayer.*
>
> 1 Timothy 4:4-5

It's a doctrine of the devil to forbid people to eat certain meats. Some may ask, "What about the Old Testament laws that forbid shellfish, pork, and other foods?" Colossians 2:16-17 says that all of those things were just shadows of something that was to come, *"but the body is of Christ."* They were just shadows.

> *Let no man therefore judge you in meat, or in drink, or in respect of an holyday, or of the new moon, or of the sabbath days: Which are a shadow of things to come; but the body is of Christ.*
>
> Colossians 2:16-17

If you were standing near me but had something blocking your view so you couldn't see me, then seeing my shadow would be beneficial to give you an idea of what I'm doing. My shadow could tell you whether I was standing still, moving toward you, moving away from you, or maybe carrying a big club. But if nothing was blocking me, and I was in full view, something would be wrong with you if you ran up and tried to shake hands with my shadow or hug my shadow.

My shadow is only beneficial when you can't see me. Once I'm in view, you can forget the shadow. Go with the real deal. This is exactly what Colossians 2:16-17 is saying. The Sabbath, partaking of certain meat and drinks, and observing certain days were all shadows of things that should come, *"but the body is of Christ."*

This is the only time in Scripture that we are told why the Old Testament dietary laws were given, and it was so they could be shadows of New Testament realities. They themselves were not the reality, and if you were to forbid people to eat certain meat based on Old Testament dietary laws, then you would be worshiping and hugging the shadow and missing the reality in Christ.

The Sabbath Was a Shadow

The Sabbath was also simply a shadow of a New Testament reality. Today, if you observe a particular day of the week as being a Sabbath day and you won't do certain things on this day, you are worshiping the shadow; you've missed the reality. Hebrews 4 tells us what the Old Testament Law was symbolic of (and today we live in): the Sabbath that Jesus provided.

> *For we which have believed do enter into rest, as he said, As I have sworn in my wrath, if they shall enter into my rest: although the works were finished from the foundation*

of the world. For he spake in a certain place of the seventh day on this wise, And God did rest the seventh day from all his works. And in this place again, If they shall enter into my rest. Seeing therefore it remaineth that some must enter therein, and they to whom it was first preached entered not in because of unbelief: Again, he limiteth a certain day, saying in David, To day, after so long a time; as it is said, To day if ye will hear his voice, harden not your hearts. For if Jesus had given them rest, then would he not afterward have spoken of another day. There remaineth therefore a rest to the people of God. For he that is entered into his rest, he also hath ceased from his own works, as God did from his.

Hebrews 4:3-10

Those who are resting in the Lord and trusting in His grace live in the real Sabbath and are the Sabbath keepers, not those who observe a certain day of the week.

People who observe particular days and are dogmatic about it and promote it are actually Sabbath breakers. I know I cause controversy for saying this because these people think that they are the ones observing the Sabbath. But the Sabbath was a picture of a New Testament reality with Jesus. Legalistic people are not resting in the Lord and trusting in His finished work; therefore, they are breaking the Sabbath.

These are all things that can sear our consciences: lies, hypocrisy, doctrines of devils, and not trusting in the Lord's finished work. So far, we've learned that our consciences can be seared and defiled. In the next chapter, we'll discover how they can also become evil.

CHAPTER 7

Why the Law?

Let us draw near with a true heart in full assurance of faith, having our hearts sprinkled from an evil conscience, and our bodies washed with pure water.

Hebrews 10:22

Based on this verse, it's evident that we can have an evil conscience and that we can be purged from that evil conscience. But how do our consciences become evil to begin with? I believe that 2 Corinthians 10:12 provides the answer:

For we dare not make ourselves of the number, or compare ourselves with some that commend themselves: but they measuring themselves by themselves, and comparing themselves among themselves, are not wise.

This passage is saying that we can skew the judgment of our consciences by comparing ourselves to one another. I believe that this is how most people arrive at their standard of right and wrong. We have an intuitive knowledge called the conscience, but Scripture says that we can defile it and sear it. And we've known from experience that it's not a totally reliable guide.

A lot of people establish their standard of morality by looking at those around them and taking an average of what they see. If they see themselves as average compared to others, they consider that to be okay.

Unfortunately, Christians do the same thing. They look to society to determine what's okay for them. For example, at one time, adultery was considered a horrible thing to do. I admit that many Christians went overboard, condemning people and treating them like trash if they'd committed adultery, and because of that, there was a backlash. But now it's gotten to the point where the divorce rate and the rate of adultery in the church are nearly identical to that of the world.

The problem is that Christians are not primarily controlled by the Word of God. They watch television shows containing immorality, and eventually these shows affect their standard of right and wrong. I remember when a television show called *Three's Company* was on. I never watched the show, but I heard that the premise was that one guy was living with two different girls. And many, many Christians watched it because it was a comedy.

If we're watching something that is an abomination to God, it will affect our consciences. When we can laugh at and love what

God hates, it affects our consciences. Since the conscience can be defiled, it cannot be our absolute guide. But, at the same time, we can't just ignore our consciences, because that's also to our detriment.

So, how do we deal with this? Paul said that he exercised himself *"to have always a conscience void of offence"* (Acts 24:16). In Acts 23:1-2, when he was standing before the Roman rulers, he said that he always had a conscience and that he had not violated his conscience. The high priest then had somebody strike him, because he believed that it was impossible for Paul to not violate his conscience. But Paul lived with a conscience that didn't give him offense. That's the way we should live. We shouldn't ignore our consciences, but at the same time, we can't let a weak conscience or a conscience that has been skewed by comparing ourselves with others become our guide.

I'm Okay. You're Okay.

I believe God gave us a conscience so that we would have an awareness of right and wrong on the inside of us. This, in turn, would show us our need for Him, bringing us to our knees and causing us to call out to Him for help. But our consciences can be defiled or seared or become evil. So, God gave us the Law to bring our consciences back to a proper place, back to the way He intended for them to function.

For the most part, religion hasn't understood this. Religion thought the reason God said "Thou shalt not . . ." was because He wanted people to fulfill all of His commands in order to be right with Him. But no one can keep the Law. No one, except Jesus, has ever kept the Law. That's a radical statement to some people!

Some of you are probably thinking, *God gave the Law for us to keep it.* No, He didn't. You can't keep the Law. Those of you who think you can are missing the whole purpose of it. The Law wasn't given for you to keep. It was given to show you God's standard of morality and perfection. If you would yield to it, it would instantly cause your conscience to start functioning right and get it back on track, showing you what the right standard is.

Second Corinthians 10:12 says that when we compare ourselves among ourselves and measure ourselves by ourselves, it's not wise. Imagine that we're standing in quicksand and sinking, but there are others in the same quicksand who are also sinking at the same rate. Many people would feel as though they were still doing okay, since they were no worse off than anyone else. That's what's happening in the church today. We look around, and everyone else seems to be living the same way we are, and because everyone else is sinking at the same rate, we don't recognize how deadly things are.

But if there was a marker of some kind on solid ground, even though everyone was sinking at the same rate, we could look at the marker and realize how much trouble we were really in. We need something immovable as a reference point.

The Ten Commandments, the Law that God gave, were His immovable standards of right and wrong. The reason God gave them to us was to activate our consciences and bring us back from having a seared conscience, an evil conscience, a defiled conscience, and a conscience that has been affected by comparing ourselves with other people.

The Ten Commandments: Good or Bad?

But if the ministration of death, written and engraven in stones, was glorious, so that the children of Israel could not stedfastly behold the face of Moses for the glory of his countenance; which glory was to be done away: How shall not the ministration of the spirit be rather glorious? For if the ministration of condemnation be glory, much more doth the ministration of righteousness exceed in glory.

2 Corinthians 3:7-9

The Law was given to show us right and wrong and to condemn us. The Law wasn't given to set us free. The *"ministration of death, written and engraven in stones"* spoken of in verse 7 is referring to the Ten Commandments. I've heard some people say that there was a ceremonial law, and then there was the Ten Commandments law, and they separate the two. They argue that the ceremonial law has been fulfilled, so we no longer have to observe the Passover or certain dietary laws, and we no longer have to do the symbolic things mentioned in the ceremonial law. But they claim that we still have to observe the Ten Commandments because we are still under that law.

The only part of the Old Testament Law that was written and engraved on stones (verse 7) was the Ten Commandments (Ex. 31:18). It was the Ten Commandments that God gave Moses on Mount Sinai, and He actually wrote them with His finger and put them in stone. This is what 2 Corinthians 3:7 is talking about.

Verse 8 says that the Old Testament Law has been superseded in the New Testament. We are not bound to the Old Testament

Law. The Old Testament Law is a ministration of death and a ministration of condemnation.

In the New Testament, Jesus came to give us life. Satan came to give us death. Satan is the one who steals, kills, and destroys, but Jesus came to give us life and give it to us more abundantly (John 10:10). Romans 8:1 says that *"there is . . . no condemnation to them which are in Christ Jesus, who walk not after the flesh, but after the Spirit."* Condemnation in the New Testament is always from the devil. Jesus isn't the one condemning us, but the Law was a ministration of condemnation.

Paul also said in 1 Corinthians 15:56 that *"the sting of death is sin; and the strength of sin is the law."* The Law strengthens sin. The Law didn't strengthen you in your battle against sin; it strengthened sin in its battle against you.

Most Christians think that God gave the Law to help us. It only helps if we have skewed or defiled consciences (Titus 1:15), have been comparing ourselves to others (2 Cor. 10:12), or have seared consciences (1 Tim. 4:2) where we lower our standards to such a degree that basically anything goes. If this is the case, then when God said, *"Thou shalt not . . . ,"* it was meant to bring our consciences back to where they are supposed to be, and that's helpful.

But we also see how the conscience condemns us, kills us, and causes shame and fear—just like it did with Adam and Eve the moment they ate of the tree and received a conscience. They began to suffer from all of its negative effects.

At the time of the Flood, the world was in such bad shape. If God didn't give the Law that would bring our consciences back to center and put us in the right place, there literally would not have been a virgin left on earth who could have given birth to Jesus. That's not an exaggeration. That's how bad things were during that time.

In Luke 17:26, Jesus said, *"As it was in the days of* [Noah], *so shall it be also in the days of the* [coming of the] *Son of man"* (brackets added). All kinds of perversion was the rule of the day back then. The cities of Sodom and Gomorrah were given over to homosexuality (Gen. 19:4-5). It was only about 2,000 years from the creation of the world to the destruction of Sodom and Gomorrah. A few hundred years later, God gave the Law to Israel. Since Sodom and Gomorrah, it's been almost 4,000 years—twice as long—and we're just now approaching the level of sin in the earth that was rampant at that time. You know what the difference was? The Law. It brought people's consciences back to a proper state.

It was necessary for God to give the Law and activate the conscience, but the conscience also condemns. The conscience doesn't ever tell you anything good. If you did ninety-nine things right and one thing wrong, your conscience would only show you the one thing you did wrong. It'll never tell you that you're doing better or you're getting closer. The conscience was given to condemn.

Under the New Covenant, we have something better, but we still need the conscience today. Some might say, "Well, then, praise God, since we're under the New Testament, maybe we should take the Ten Commandments off the walls and remove them from public places because now we've got a greater law, something better."

The difference is that not everyone is saved and following the Spirit of God. For people who don't know God, their consciences are the only restraint that they have against ungodliness. We need the Law. We need to have this perfect standard for our lives. Non-Christians need to know God's standard of right and wrong and what is godly and ungodly. Because of this, we should keep the Ten Commandments in public places. God didn't change His standard; He just fulfilled it.

Guilty

It is wrong to think that God gave us the Law so that by keeping it, we could somehow earn a relationship with Him. Our "cleanness" before God is not based on our adherence to the Law. The Law doesn't make us right with God; it amplifies the conscience and brings it back to a proper standard. Romans 3 describes the Law's purpose:

There is none righteous, no, not one.

Romans 3:10

Now we know that what things soever the law saith, it saith to them who are under the law: that every mouth may be stopped, and all the world may become guilty before God.

Romans 3:19

For all have sinned, and come short of the glory of God.

Romans 3:23

The Law was given to stop your mouth or, in other words, to stop your excuses. People may say "I've done wrong, but I was raised in an abusive family" and so on. Then they blame everyone else for the bad things they do. The Law does not give allowances for why you did what you did. If you broke the standard, you're guilty; it doesn't show mercy. So, the Law brought your conscience back and stopped your excuses, making you guilty before God.

This is exactly what happened to Adam and Eve when they sinned; immediately they were guilty (Gen. 3:7-10). They were afraid God would judge them, so they hid themselves. This is the working of the conscience. Romans 3:20 explains how the Law gives us knowledge of sin: *"Therefore by the deeds of the law there shall no flesh be justified in his sight: for by the law is the knowledge of sin."* The purpose of the Law is to amplify the conscience and show you whether you were right or wrong.

Romans 7:5 explains how sin gained traction and access to us through the Law: *"For when we were in the flesh, the motions of sins, which were by the law, did work in our members to bring forth fruit unto death."* Continuing in verses 6-7, we see that the Law actually made sin come alive.

> ***But now we are delivered from the law, that being dead wherein we were held; that we should serve in newness of spirit, and not in the oldness of the letter. What shall we say then? Is the law sin? God forbid.***
>
> **Romans 7:6-7a**

Some may reason that because the Law kills, condemns, strengthens sin, and makes us guilty, it is all bad. But it was actually good at the time it was given. People must be brought back to their need for God, and the conscience does that. It shows us that we've

fallen short and makes us fearful and guilt-ridden. This is good as long as we don't stay there, but rather use it to motivate us toward God and receive forgiveness.

Unfortunately, many people don't understand these things, and they allow their consciences to condemn them and keep them in a constant state of unworthiness, sin, and unforgiveness. The Law itself isn't sin, but it's necessary to bring us to a place of recognizing our need for God. In the following chapter, we'll see how the Law actually draws us toward sin.

CHAPTER 8

The Law Brings Sin to Life

Once, when I was ministering in Houston, Texas, at a Holiday Inn, a man walked past the doors of the room we were in and just stood outside watching. Finally, he came inside but just stood at the back of the room and listened for a while. Then he started speaking while I was preaching. What he said was incoherent, so I asked him a couple of questions.

After a while it was obvious that he was just there to interrupt the meeting, and I realized that there was a demonic presence in him. I looked right at him and said, "I command you to sit down and shut up in the name of Jesus," and he just plopped right down. So, I went ahead and finished preaching, and after the service ended, I started talking to this man. I began telling him about the love of God, and

I said, "God loves you. God wants to set you free from whatever it is that's binding you." And I just began to minister grace to him.

Instead of receiving that, he responded by saying, "I don't need God. I am God." I think he must have been drunk or high on something, and he kept proclaiming, "I am God." Obviously, he was deceived, and he needed to be brought out of his deception. At that point, I reverted to the Law. I had been telling him about the love of God and the grace of God, but once he started saying he *was* God, I used the Word to knock some sense into the guy. I said, "You think you're God? You sorry thing! You're a stench in God's nostrils."

I began to show him things he was doing wrong, and within moments, this man's conscience came back to him. He began crying and said, "Oh God, have mercy on me!" He realized his need for God.

Ray Comfort illustrates the use of the Law very well. I've seen his videos where he goes up to college students and asks them if they are going to heaven. Most of them say they are. Then Ray asks them why they think that. They usually give some answer along the lines of them being a good person.

Next, Ray asks them, "Have you ever lied?" They admit they have, and then Ray shows them Revelation 21:8, which says:

> *But the fearful, and unbelieving, and the abominable, and murderers, and whoremongers, and sorcerers, and idolaters,*

> *and all liars, shall have their part in the lake which burneth with fire and brimstone: which is the second death.*

Then Ray asks them, "Have you ever lusted after someone?" Of course, they say they have, and he shows them the scripture that says lusting after someone is the same as committing adultery (Matt. 5:27-28). Then Ray says something like, "Have you ever hated someone? The Bible compares that to murder (Matt. 5:21-22)."

After Ray uses the Law, the people recognize they have sinned. Their consciences are brought back to center, rightly condemning them and showing them their need for a Savior.

I use this story to further illustrate the purpose of the Law, as I began discussing in the last chapter. The Law shows you your ungodliness and brings you to the end of yourself so that you have to call out to God.

> *But we know that the law is good, if a man use it lawfully; Knowing this, that the law is not made for a righteous man, but for the lawless and disobedient.*
>
> **1 Timothy 1:8-9a**

The Law isn't made for Christians; Christians aren't supposed to be relating to God based on dos and don'ts and how well they measure up. There's a different way for New Testament believers to relate to God. Under the New Covenant, we have something better than the Law and the conscience:

> *But now the righteousness of God without the law is manifested, being witnessed by the law and the prophets; Even*

> *the righteousness of God which is by faith of Jesus Christ unto all and upon all them that believe: for there is no difference.*
>
> Romans 3:21-22

For those who have not yet committed themselves to God, though, the Law was given to make sin come alive on the inside of them, and there is a godly purpose for that.

We Always Want What We Can't Have

> *What shall we say then? Is the law sin? God forbid. Nay, I had not known sin, but by the law: for I had not known lust, except the law had said, Thou shalt not covet. But sin, taking occasion by the commandment, wrought in me all manner of concupiscence. For without the law sin was dead.*
>
> Romans 7:7-8

Our consciences would not function properly if God hadn't given us His standard of morality. The Law taught us right from wrong. The word *concupiscence* in verse 8 means "'a desire, craving, longing, mostly of evil desires,' frequently translated 'lust'" (*Vine's Expository Dictionary of Old and New Testament Words*). Did you know that the Law actually draws you to sin through condemnation? God didn't create us to live by dos and don'ts. He created Adam and Eve to live in freedom.

There's something inside of us that longs to be free and hates restriction and limitations. When the Law says "Thou shalt not," it makes us lust for the very thing that it tells us we can't have. Even if you didn't like chocolate, I could say, "I'll give you a million dollars if you can go one year without eating chocolate or even wanting chocolate." Before long, you would be thinking about it and lusting for it, and me telling you that you can't have it would make you want it more.

Did you know the Law makes you more vulnerable to sin? Romans 7:9 goes on to say, *"For I was alive without the law once: but when the commandment came, sin revived, and I died."* The Law, contrary to what people think, didn't diminish sin; it actually made sin come alive.

Born into Sin

When you were born, you had a sin nature. It's not your sins that made you a sinner. You were born with a sin nature. Everyone is born separated from God. When David said *"in sin did my mother conceive me"* (Ps. 51:5), he wasn't talking about an illegitimate conception. He was just saying that he was born a sinner.

Paul confirmed this in Ephesians 2:3 when he said that we *"were by nature the children of wrath."* We were all born sinners. A toddler has a sin nature. If you don't believe me, just watch one. They have no problem thinking only about themselves, taking something from someone else, throwing a fit, hurting others, or criticizing others. Children don't have to be taught to be bad; it's in their nature. They were born with a sin nature, but according to Romans 5:13, *"sin is not imputed when there is no law."*

The word *impute* basically means to charge to your account or hold against you. When children are born, they have a sin nature, which you can see the effects of. But if children die before the Law makes their consciences come alive, their sin would not be imputed to them. They would go to heaven, even though they had sinned, because they hadn't knowingly activated that sin on the inside of them.

Some people are born with mental disabilities, and they could be thirty or forty years old and still not have sin come alive on the inside of them. Their sin nature wouldn't be imputed to them because they don't have the mental faculties to understand what's going on.

In 2 Samuel 12:23, when David's son died, David said, *"I shall go to him, but he shall not return to me."* David wasn't going to hell; he was going into the presence of God, where his child was. David said that when his child died, he went into the presence of the Lord. There are certain sects, like the Catholic Church and some others, that baptize infants. They do this to deal with this original sin, or the sin nature. The only problem is that the baptism is just a formality; it doesn't do anything. Infant baptism doesn't mean a blooming thing, and it can't be found anywhere in Scripture.

In Acts 8:35-37, the Ethiopian eunuch heard Philip preaching. The eunuch basically said to Philip, "Here's some water. What would keep me from being baptized?" Philip responded, "If you believe with all of your heart, you may."

You have to believe with all of your heart, which means you have to be old enough to rationalize and understand what's going on for baptism to do any good. It's true that children are born with a sin nature, but that sin nature isn't held against them until they knowingly violate their consciences. Once the Law comes alive, their consciences revive. Then when they violate their consciences, that is when they're held accountable for their sin nature.

The first time that I remember the Law coming alive in my life (and it's possible that it happened before this), I was eight years old. I realized I hadn't just violated my parents' instructions by disobeying them, but I had also sinned against God. When I saw that, fear hit me. Sin came alive in me, and the next day I got born again.

Never Good Enough

If you understand that we all have a sin nature and a conscience but that God gave us the Law so our consciences would come alive, it will totally change the way you relate to God.

> *But we know that the law is good, if a man use it lawfully; Knowing this, that the law is not made for a righteous man, but for the lawless and disobedient, for the ungodly and for sinners, for unholy and profane, for murderers of fathers and murderers of mothers, for manslayers, For whoremongers, for them that defile themselves with mankind, for menstealers, for*

liars, for perjured persons, and if there be any other thing that is contrary to sound doctrine.

1 Timothy 1:8-10

The Law was not made for a righteous person, or someone who is born again. The Law is not for New Testament believers. Religion preaches the Law as being our savior; if you do this and this and this, then God will bless you. That's not the purpose of the Law. The Law was given to show you that you're incapable of ever fulfilling it.

A lot of people honestly believe that if their good deeds outweigh the bad, then God will accept them. They believe that although they're not perfect, if they are relatively good, then God will accept them. But that's not what God says:

For whosoever shall keep the whole law, and yet offend in one point, he is guilty of all.

James 2:10

God doesn't grade on a curve. He doesn't accept you if you're better than somebody else or if you're making a passing grade. You either have to be perfect, or you need a Savior. God raises the bar so high that no one can ever reach His standard. Nobody can live perfectly according to the Law, but that's the point of why it was given: to prove that we're incapable of saving ourselves so that we'd have to throw ourselves on the mercy of God.

A friend of mine told a story about a guy who went to heaven, and when he got there, Peter met him at the gate. Peter said, "You've got to take this test, and you've got to get 100 points on the test before we'll let you in." The guy said, "No problem. I've been a Christian my whole life. I've gone to church. I'm a good person. I can get 100 points, no problem."

The first question was, "Did you go to church?" The guy said, "I never missed church." He showed Peter all of his attendance pins and said, "I had perfect attendance." Peter said, "Okay, that's worth half of a point." Next question was, "Were you faithful to your wife?" The man responds, "Yeah, I never cheated on my wife." Peter said, "Well, that's worth one point." Then Peter asks, "Did you tithe?" The guy said, "Yes, I tithed." Again, Peter said, "Okay, that's worth half of a point."

After about five or six questions, the man only had three points. Finally, he said, "My God, if this is what you demand, have mercy on me!" Peter replied, "Come on in!"

Peter was trying to get him to come to the end of himself. That's exactly why the Law was given. We have to realize that *"all have sinned, and come short of the glory of God"* (Rom. 3:23). We need to quit trusting in our self-righteousness and look to God for salvation. If the Law is used for this purpose, it's good.

There's still a right use of the Law today for our lawless society, which says that anything and everything goes. People today don't feel like they need to be forgiven because they don't see what's wrong with having sex with somebody of the same sex, "shacking up" with people, lying or stealing, and so forth. God had to do something to bring our consciences back to a state of understanding right and wrong, so He gave us the Law.

If people had this knowledge of right and wrong, you wouldn't see them flaunting their sins. You wouldn't see people committing murder and then killing themselves and thinking they just got by with something. They'd recognize that they didn't get by with anything but rather just ushered themselves into a Christ-less eternity where they'll suffer forever.

People need to realize that they are sinners so they can come to the end of themselves.

But then once they do and they begin following the Lord, they are no longer under that schoolmaster. Now they have to deal with their consciences that condemn them. Let's look now at how God says New Testament believers should deal with their consciences and relate to Him.

CHAPTER 9

A Better Way

Have you ever wondered if the Law was God's first choice? Why didn't He just give Adam and Eve a long list of things to do and not to do? The reason is because He didn't want them living a life of condemnation.

Adam and Eve ate of the Tree of the Knowledge of Good and Evil. Immediately, they recognized they were naked, so they sewed fig leaves together and hid themselves. Out of all the consequences their disobedience brought about, being naked was one of the least of these consequences. If the Lord had shown them all that would happen as a result of their disobedience—murder within their own family, entire cities given over to homosexuality, all but eight people on earth wiped out in a flood, a holocaust, and world wars—Adam and Eve wouldn't have been able to bear it. So, He didn't show them.

They didn't understand the depth of their sin; they just knew they were naked. They knew something was wrong, but they couldn't comprehend it all. God used to speak to them face to face, so He could have explained it to them. But He didn't want them feeling condemned.

The problem was that, over time, people began to take God's lack of punishment and intervention as approval of their sin. They deadened themselves to their conscience, thinking that things weren't that bad. This is evident in Genesis 4:8-15, where Cain killed Abel. Instead of God venting His wrath, He protected Cain.

God set a mark on him and said, "If anybody touches Cain, I will avenge him sevenfold." God protected the first murderer on the face of the earth! There were consequences to what Cain did, but God didn't unleash the fullness of His wrath on him. Instead, He responded in mercy. James 2:13 says that *"mercy rejoiceth against judgment."* God wanted to operate in mercy toward the human race.

Later in Genesis 4, verses 23-24, Cain's great-great-great-grandson Lamech killed a man in self-defense:

> ***I have slain a man to my wounding, and a young man to my hurt. If Cain shall be avenged sevenfold, truly Lamech seventy and sevenfold.***

Lamech said that if God avenged Cain sevenfold, God will avenge him seventy and sevenfold. In other words, in Lamech's mind, his murder was justified. It was more justifiable than Cain's, so if Cain got by with murder, he figured he'd get by with murder. What's wrong with Lamech's statement is that God didn't say that. Lamech just assumed that would be God's response.

Because God wasn't intervening and punishing and judging mankind, murder became commonplace, and sexual immorality was running rampant. The earth was spinning out of control with sin. So finally, God had to give the Law. But He waited two thousand years to do so because He didn't want us to know how vile we really were.

You Can't Reason with a Toddler

If you have children, you don't want to have to spank or punish them. Some parents say, "I love my kids too much to spank or correct them." But Proverbs 19:18 says, *"Chasten thy son while there is hope."* The Bible tells us that if we don't chasten our kids, we hate them (Prov. 13:24). If you love your kids, you will restrain them.

But you can't restrain a young child through reason. You can't tell your child, "If you take someone's toy, you're operating in selfishness. God is a giver, so you're submitting yourself to the devil. According to John 10:10, Satan is going to steal, kill, and destroy, and you'll never have friends. Nobody will like you because you're selfish. If you get a job, you'll wind up getting fired because you aren't thinking about being responsible and doing what's right. If you ever get married, your marriage will fall apart."

You can't tell a child this; children don't have a clue what all that means. But you can tell a toddler, "If you do that again, I'll spank you." And even though children don't know about God or the devil and heaven or hell, they do know there are consequences to doing what's wrong.

You can get a toddler to resist the devil and resist temptation to be selfish through fear of punishment. This is what the Law was all about.

> *The natural man receiveth not the things of the Spirit of God: for they are foolishness unto him: neither can he know them, because they are spiritually discerned.*
>
> **1 Corinthians 2:14**

Before people get born again, they can't understand the things of God, similar to a little child. Under the Old Testament, a person couldn't be born again, so how did God get people who were carnal to understand that their behavior was wrong? Simple. God said, "You sin, and I'll kill you. I'll smite you with the botch, the mildew, and the emerods; your crops won't grow," and on and on (Deut. 28:15-68).

A carnal person understands that, just like a child understands. But when your children get to be twenty or thirty years old and you say, "You do that again, and I'm going to spank you," that's not going to fly. At some point you need to begin explaining to them and helping them to understand the consequences of their actions. Until that time, however, you can use corporal punishment to motivate them. That's a godly thing, and in a sense, that's what God had to do with mankind.

No Room for Error

Prior to the Law, Abraham would've broken the Law by marrying his half sister. According to Leviticus 18:9-30, if you married a half sister it was an abomination, and you were to be put to death. But instead of God judging him, Abraham *"was called the Friend of God"* (James 2:23). He was the only person in the Old Testament ever to be called the friend of God.

Later, Abraham's grandson Jacob came along and married two sisters while both were still alive (Gen. 29:23-28), which also was an abomination and cause for death. Again, instead of God judging and punishing him, Jacob wrestled with an angel and prevailed (Gen. 32:24-29). God honored him by changing his name to Israel, and he became one of the patriarchs.

In contrast, Numbers 15:32-36 gives an account of the first person who broke the Law once it was in effect. He was a man who picked up sticks on the Sabbath to make a fire to cook food. Because he broke the Sabbath law, Moses locked him up until he could hear from the Lord on what to do with him. The Lord said, "Kill him; stone him to death," so the man was put to death for picking up sticks.

What a difference the Law makes! God gave the Law to activate our conscience and make sin come alive in us so that condemnation would drive us to the Lord. But God waited to enact the Law because He wanted to be merciful to our sins. He didn't want to aggravate our conscience and make it worse than it was.

God doesn't want us to be ruled by our conscience. He wants us to purge ourselves from an evil conscience and recognize that there is now a better way to relate to Him. The Law could never set us free from feeling unworthy and condemned. But, as born-again believers, the blood of Jesus can.

Out with the Old and In with the New

The book of Hebrews is a powerful book that was written to transition us from a Law-based relationship, where we related to God based on our performance, to where we relate to Him based on what Jesus has done for us. In chapter 9, comparisons are made between the way things were done under the Old Testament and the way God deals with us under the New Testament. First, let's look at verse 9, which talks about Old Testament sacrifices:

> *Which was a figure for the time then present, in which were offered both gifts and sacrifices, that could not make him that did the service perfect, as pertaining to the conscience.*
>
> **Hebrews 9:9**

The Old Covenant could never purge the conscience, but the New Covenant can:

> *How much more shall the blood of Christ, who through the eternal Spirit offered himself without spot to God, purge your conscience from dead works to serve the living God?"*
>
> **Hebrews 9:14**

Under the New Covenant, we can live lives free of sin-consciousness, which is a blasphemous statement to many Christians. The blood of Jesus can purge our consciences from dead works. It will purge us from feeling as though we have to do something to earn things from God, like being worthy enough to get our prayers answered or living holy so God will move in our lives. These things are dead works that we have to be purged from in order to serve the living God. We cannot truly serve God if we are sin conscious.

Hebrews 10:1-2 asks a question: *"For the law having a shadow of good things to come, and not the very image of the things, can never with those sacrifices which they offered year by year continually make the comers thereunto perfect. For then would they not have ceased to be offered?"* If the Old Testament sacrifices worked, then wouldn't people have been able to quit offering them? But they never worked, so people had to offer them over and over again.

The Old Testament sacrifices never set anyone free from anything; they were only pictures, shadows, and types of what would happen through the atonement of the Lord Jesus. The type and shadow had to be kept in front of people so they could continually realize their need for the atonement of their sins.

Hebrews 10:2 continues, *"because that the worshippers once purged should have had no more conscience of sins."* If the Old Testament sacrifices really worked, they would have eliminated sin-consciousness, or the "conscience of sins"—the conscience condemning us. Since the New Testament sacrifice of Jesus did work, Christians should not have any consciousness of sin. That is one huge statement. I've never heard another living, breathing person ever say that. Most people are afraid to make this statement. They're afraid that if we quit being conscious of sin, there won't be anything to restrain us, because they use fear as a motivator.

Love, however, is a stronger motivator than fear. We can get to the place where we are so captivated by the love of God that His love will constrain us. Paul said that the love of Christ constrained him (2 Cor. 5:14). We can get to where we serve God out of love, not out of fear of punishment and rejection. Yet most Christians—I would daresay more than 90 percent of all Christians—serve God out of obligation, debt, and fear, not out of love.

First John 4:18 states that *"fear hath torment. He that feareth is not made perfect in love."* Most Christians serve God out of fear of rejection. They read their Bible, not because they love it and they love God, but out of obligation. It's like they're saying, "God, I've read the Bible. Now You've got to do something for me."

I had a woman tell me recently that she heard my teaching *A Better Way to Pray,* and through it, she was set free from all of the rules and regulations about having to spend a certain amount of time in prayer and Bible reading. Now she just worships the Lord and prays all day long instead of jumping through religious hoops where prayer is concerned. I'm not against prayer, but I am against the concept that prayer somehow makes God move or that it suddenly makes you holy. And as a result, God will answer you because you've spent so much time praying. Those are dead works.

For us to truly enter the holy of holies—the very presence of God—and have an intimate relationship with Him, we must purge our conscience from dead works and from an evil conscience.

> *Having therefore, brethren, boldness to enter into the holiest by the blood of Jesus, by a new and living way, which he hath consecrated for us, through the veil, that is to say, his flesh; and having an high priest over the house of God; let us draw near with a true heart in full assurance of faith, having our hearts sprinkled from an evil conscience, and our bodies washed with pure water.*
>
> Hebrews 10:19-22

Jesus and Religion Don't Mix

Most Christians still have a sin-consciousness, and this is where they miss it. Unfortunately, the vast majority of religion today is based on preaching the Law and not grace. There is a place for preaching the Law, because if people don't recognize their need for the Lord, they need the Law to activate their conscience and come to the end of themselves so they'll turn to Jesus and become born again.

As mentioned earlier, 1 Timothy 1:9 says, *"The law is not made for a righteous man, but for the lawless and disobedient."* But once a person is born again, the Law is counterproductive to having an intimate and personal relationship with God because all it does is minister guilt and condemnation. That's what Hebrews 9 and 10 explain.

Many Christians still haven't moved into the New Covenant and are trying to mix Old Testament Law with New Testament grace. Jesus said you can't put new wine into an old wineskin because when the wine ferments and expands, the wineskin will burst. Likewise, no one puts a new patch on an old garment because when the patch shrinks, the garment will tear (Matt. 9:16-17). You can't put the New Testament wine that Jesus provided into the Old Testament wineskin of the Law. They are incompatible.

Jesus was crucified because the religious leaders of His day were under the Law and condemnation. The religious leaders thought that the way to get people close to God was to tell them how unworthy they were so they groveled and begged God for mercy. They hated Jesus for forgiving the prostitute, eating at the publican's house, and entering the Pharisee's house. They hated Him because He violated their religious tradition. They constantly accused Him of breaking the Law. Jesus never did, but He broke their interpretation of the Law.

The religious system of the day is what persecuted, condemned, and killed Jesus. The Romans would've let Him go. Pilate would have let Him go (John 19:12). Religion is what killed Jesus. Religion today is when the Law is proclaimed. Religion is the number one practice on earth that preaches the Law and puts Christians under condemnation. Once people have repented, they don't need to stay condemned under the Law. The blood of Jesus has provided us with a much better way to relate to God.

CHAPTER 10

Come on In!

Then verily the first covenant [talking about the Law] *had also ordinances of divine service, and a worldly sanctuary. For there was a tabernacle made; the first, wherein was the candlestick, and the table, and the shewbread; which is called the sanctuary. And after the second veil, the tabernacle which is called the Holiest of all; which had the golden censer, and the ark of the covenant overlaid round about with gold, wherein was the golden pot that had manna, and Aaron's rod that budded, and the tables of the covenant; and over it the cherubims of glory shadowing the mercyseat; of which we cannot now speak particularly.*

Hebrews 9:1-5, brackets added

When Moses was on Mount Sinai for forty days and forty nights (Ex. 24:18), God gave him the Ten Commandments and he saw the temple of God that was in heaven. The temple had three parts: an outer court, an inner court, and the holy of holies. After Moses saw all of this, he came down off the mountain, and in Exodus 40:16-33, he made a tabernacle out of tents and curtains that mimicked the temple that God had shown him in heaven.

The tabernacle, along with the temple that Solomon built in 1 Chronicles 28:11-19, was modeled after something that is a reality in heaven. There is a real temple in heaven. God had Moses reproduce it; everything that he made in the tabernacle imitated something that is actually in the temple in heaven. Everything had a symbolic meaning in order to depict how we relate to God.

This is what the author of Hebrews was talking about in chapter 9, verses 1-5. There was the first tabernacle, then the holy place, and then the holy of holies. Inside were a candlestick, the table, the shewbread, and so forth. All of these things apply to us in our relationship with God today. They all have a direct application until verse 5, which says, *"Over it the cherubims of glory shadowing the mercyseat; of which we cannot now speak particularly."*

In other words, everything else had an application for us today, but these cherubim, or angels, do not apply to us today; we can't speak about that today. This is referring to God's presence in the ark of the covenant. In the movie *Raiders of the Lost Ark*, they open up the ark, and the angels kill everybody and everything.

Of course, that's Hollywood's interpretation of what could happen, but it is true that if a person even touched the ark they would die. In 2 Samuel 6:6-7, the oxen carrying the ark stumbled, so Uzzah touched the ark to try to steady it. But God struck him dead for touching it:

> *And when they came to Nachon's threshingfloor, Uzzah put forth his hand to the ark of God, and took hold of it; for the oxen shook it. And the anger of the* Lord *was kindled against Uzzah; and God smote him there for his error; and there he died by the ark of God.*

You couldn't come near the ark, because that was the presence of God. The mercy seat was where God sat. In the Old Covenant, there was a veil separating the place where the priest went and the holy place where God dwelt. Over it were the cherubim. In the original ark that Moses made, there were two little golden cherubim that stretched their wings toward each other and touched in the middle over the mercy seat.

Angels Aren't Fat Little Babies

Solomon's temple was ninety feet long, thirty feet wide, and forty-five feet high (1 Kin. 6:2). The cherubim in his temple were so huge that one wing touched one wall, the other wing touched the other angel's wing, and then that angel's other wing touched another wall. So, the cherubim had their wings spread and covered the entire holy of holies. If anyone went into the holy of holies except the high priest once a year, God struck that person dead. Even the high priest had to go through a complicated system of making himself pure and making offerings for himself. And if he didn't do everything properly, God would strike him dead as well.

Josephus, a first-century historian who wrote about the history of the Jews for the Romans, said that the high priest would go into the holy of holies with a rope tied around his ankle that was allowed to drag out into the holy place. That way, if the priest who went in was defiled and God struck him dead, he could be pulled out. Otherwise, whoever went in after him would also be struck dead.

It would definitely sober you up to have to go in with a rope around your foot, knowing that if everything wasn't just right, God would kill you. But who actually killed those who went in defiled? It was the cherubim. Cherubim aren't fat little babies! In Genesis 3:22-24, God set warrior angels, or cherubim, at the east end of the Garden of Eden with flaming swords to protect the path to the Tree of Life. Cherubim are mighty warrior angels.

But in Hebrews 9:5, the writer said that we can't talk about these angels now and how they killed people:

> *And over it the cherubims of glory shadowing the mercyseat; of which we cannot now speak particularly.*

Because now, the veil of the temple has been rent in two, and you and I can just stroll into the holy of holies anytime we want because of what Jesus has done.

> *And, behold, the veil of the temple was rent in twain from the top to the bottom; and the earth did quake, and the rocks rent.*
>
> Matthew 27:51

This part of the temple no longer applies to us. The veil has been torn in two; the cherubim are gone. If an angel came between you and God when you were about to worship the Lord and said,

"Stop! What makes you worthy?" you could rebuke him in the name of Jesus and say, "Through the blood of Jesus I have a right to enter into the very presence of God." No angel can stop you. That is just awesome!

No More Separation

Now when these things were thus ordained, the priests went always into the first tabernacle, accomplishing the service of God. But into the second went the high priest alone once every year, not without blood, which he offered for himself, and for the errors of the people: The Holy Ghost this signifying, that the way into the holiest of all was not yet made manifest, while as the first tabernacle was yet standing.

Hebrews 9:6-8

In the Old Testament there was a separation between God and man, and the tabernacle depicted this. Later, the temple also depicted this same separation between God and man. That separation is now gone in the New Covenant. Yet if you are hearing the Law preached and being taught that you have to follow all kinds of rules and behave in a certain way in order for God to love you, accept you, and answer your prayers, then you are back to operating under an Old Testament Law mentality.

This type of mentality keeps us from intimacy with God because our conscience will once again be activated by the Law, which will cause us to be ridden with guilt and have feelings of unworthiness. Unfortunately, this is very descriptive of the average Christian.

Hebrews 9:9 says, "*Which was a figure for the time then present, in which were offered both gifts and sacrifices, that could not make him that did the service perfect, as pertaining to the conscience.*" The Old Testament Law did not set us free from an evil conscience; it gave us an evil conscience. It caused our conscience to condemn and kill ourselves.

Continuing in verse 10, the writer talks about the "time of reformation":

> *Which stood only in meats and drinks, and divers washings, and carnal ordinances, imposed on them until the time of reformation.*

This isn't referring to the reformation that Martin Luther brought about in the 1500s, but rather the reformation that came through Jesus. It was only up until the time of Jesus that all of these symbolic acts were done. Now that we're living under the New Covenant, we should have a totally different way of approaching God than the Old Testament saints had. Sadly, most Christians don't fully understand this.

Are You Insulting Jesus?

So often in our churches we sing songs of David from Psalm 51:10-11: "*Create in me a clean heart . . . and renew a right spirit within me. Cast me not away from thy presence; and take not thy holy spirit from me.*" This was fine for David because he lived under a covenant where he was separated from God. All of these things that he sang about could have actually happened.

But in the New Covenant, God says, *"I will never leave thee, nor forsake thee"* (Heb. 13:5). When we are born again, we are recreated with a brand-new heart. So, for a New Testament believer to pray this same prayer that David prayed is an insult to Jesus because it is denying the covenant that we have with God.

If we pray or sing, "Oh God, don't take Your Holy Spirit from me," like David did in Psalm 51:11, we are denying what God has said to us in Hebrews 13:5. There's no way to justify asking God to not take His Spirit from us, except through ignorance or unbelief. I can just imagine people singing this song, asking God to not take His Holy Spirit from them, and then the Father saying to Jesus, "Didn't You tell them that You would never leave them nor forsake them and that You'll be with them always?" (Matt. 28:20).

God is never going to leave us! Yet people pray prayers and sing songs that indicate that He will. In David's time, there were things that happened under the Old Testament that cannot happen today to the New Testament believer. Hebrews 9:14 says, *"How much more shall the blood of Christ, who through the eternal Spirit offered himself without spot to God, purge your conscience from dead works to serve the living God?"* Now, people who aren't New Covenant believers are still under the Old Testament Law and are subject to these things that David wrote about (John 3:36). But once you're born again, God treats you differently. You have to purge your conscience, and you have to recognize that there is a difference between the Old Testament and New Testament believer.

Sadly, the average Christian is not living under the New Covenant but is still serving God under the Old Testament Law. This brings fear of God's judgment, rejection, and punishment, which is not the way the Lord wants us to live in His presence. He wants us to come boldly to His throne to receive His unending mercy (Heb. 4:16).

In the next chapter, we'll continue in Hebrews 9 to learn what it means for us today that Jesus is our Great High Priest and discover if it's true that you can lose your salvation because of sin.

CHAPTER 11

Once for All

We've been reading in Hebrews 9 and seeing how the author contrasted the Old Covenant way of doing things with the New Covenant way of doing things. In the Old Covenant, every time a person sinned, there had to be an offering to atone for that sin. There had to be an animal sacrifice, and blood had to be shed for sin every single time a sin was committed. But under the New Covenant, Jesus entered into the holy place once and obtained eternal redemption for us.

> *But Christ being come an high priest of good things to come, by a greater and more perfect tabernacle, not made with hands, that is to say, not of this building; neither by the blood of goats and calves, but by his own blood he entered in once into the holy place, having obtained eternal redemption for us.*
>
> Hebrews 9:11-12

Ephesians 1:7 and Colossians 1:14 are very similar verses that state that we have received redemption, or the forgiveness of our sins.

> *In whom we have redemption through his blood, the forgiveness of sins, according to the riches of his grace.*
>
> Ephesians 1:7

> *In whom we have redemption through his blood, even the forgiveness of sins.*
>
> Colossians 1:14

The biblical definition of *redemption* is *the forgiveness of sins.* We just read Hebrews 9:12 telling us that Jesus entered into the holy place once to obtain eternal forgiveness of our sins. Yet many Christians think that every time they sin, it's a new offense against God—they are once again rejected and there will be varying degrees of punishment because of their sin. Some ultra-Pentecostals believe that every time Christians sin, they lose their salvation, become backslidden, and need to get born again, again.

A similar interpretation of this is that we won't necessarily lose our salvation when we sin, but we will lose our fellowship with God, and He will no longer answer our prayers or use us if we have sin in our lives. It's like having a stick with total rejection on one end and partial rejection on the other, but the whole stick still speaks of rejection. But none of this is true. God has forgiven us of all sins—past, present, and even future sins. *All* sins have been forgiven through Christ.

The veil wasn't torn in two to give us access into the holy of holies only until the next time we sin. The veil does not come back together and separate us once again from God until we put our sins under the blood. No, God forgave all of our past, present, and future sins when we were born again.

You're Going to Sin

I know some of you are thinking, *How can God forgive a sin before it's committed?* Jesus only died once for your sins 2,000 years ago. If He can't forgive a sin before you commit it, you can't be saved, because you hadn't committed any sins yet when He died for them. He died for *all* of our sins. First John 2:2 says that Jesus died for the sins of the whole world:

> *And he is the propitiation for our sins: and not for ours only, but also for the sins of the whole world.*

The atonement has already been made for the sins of the whole world. When Hebrews 9:12 tells us that Jesus *"entered in once . . . having obtained eternal redemption for us,"* this isn't talking about momentary redemption just until the next time we sin. If I really believed that every time you sin you lose your salvation, become backslidden, and have to get born again, again, I'd do you a service to kill you the moment you got saved. I might go to hell, but the only way you'd ever get to heaven is to have someone kill you right at that moment, because I can guarantee you that you will sin again.

James 4:17 says, *"To him that knoweth to do good, and doeth it not, to him it is sin."* Sin isn't only when you break the "big ten." The

Catholics categorize sins into cardinal sins versus acceptable sins, but there are no acceptable sins with God.

Look what James chapter 2 says:

> *For whosoever shall keep the whole law, and yet offend in one point, he is guilty of all.*
>
> **James 2:10**

If you believe that you could somehow or another never sin, then you don't understand that when you fail to be the person you're supposed to be, you are sinning. It's not just when you break a direct command. If husbands don't love their wives the way they're supposed to, or if wives don't reverence their husbands the way they're supposed to, then they're sinning. We may be doing better than we've ever done before, and we may be doing better than other people, but none of us is perfect; therefore, we're sinning.

None of us loves each other and thinks about others more than we think about ourselves. All of us are failing to be perfect as we're supposed to be. If you believe that by having sin in your life God won't accept you, then get saved and let me kill you immediately. That's the only way you're ever going to maintain your holiness and get to heaven.

Turkeys, Eagles, and Sin-Consciousness

This is why most Christians have no confidence or boldness in their relationship with God. They're still living under the Law and are constantly aware of their shortcomings. There was a man named Peter Lord who used to preach a message called "Turkeys & Eagles." It's a classic message about how, as Christians, we're supposed to be eagles that soar high in the sky, but instead we're turkeys that walk around on the ground and stay earthbound because we don't know who we are in Christ and what we've been forgiven of.

One Sunday morning at an eight o'clock service, Peter Lord asked the congregation, "How many people in here sinned this morning?" Every person raised a hand. Peter's wife was sitting in the front row, and even she raised her hand. He asked her, "What have you done? It's only eight o'clock in the morning."

His wife said, "Well, I can't really think of anything, but I know I'm constantly falling short. I know I've done something wrong!" Peter used that as an illustration of how we live with a sin-consciousness and a sense of unworthiness. He continued by asking, "Why don't you think about what you've done well? You woke up and took a shower. That's good!"

I go places where people don't ever take showers and never clean their clothes. Let me tell you, it's a good thing that you get clean and smell nice. Amen! Peter's point was that you brushed your teeth, you combed your hair, you put on clothes; you've done a lot of good things, but instead of seeing the good you do, you live under a sin-consciousness. If someone asks, "How many of you have sinned today?" even if you can't think of something you did, you'd raise your hand because you just know you've done something wrong.

Sin-consciousness comes because of the Law. Hebrews 10:2 tells us that we *"should have . . . no more conscience of sins."* It doesn't say "no more consciousness," but rather *"no more conscience of sins."* There's a difference. This means that your conscience should not condemn you if you understand Jesus's atonement.

We learned in Hebrews 9:12 that through one offering we have been forgiven of all sins—past, present, and even future sins. Continue reading in verses 13-14:

> *For if the blood of bulls and of goats, and the ashes of an heifer sprinkling the unclean, sanctifieth to the purifying of the flesh* **[talking about if the Old Testament symbols could actually do something to affect you spiritually]**, *How much more shall the blood of Christ, who through the eternal Spirit offered himself without spot to God, purge your conscience from dead works to serve the living God?*
>
> **Hebrews 9:13-14, brackets added**

The Old Testament Law couldn't really do anything. Hebrews 9:9 says that it couldn't perfect the person according to the conscience. But the blood of the Lord Jesus can purge your conscience from dead works so you can serve the living God. If your conscience isn't purged, you can't serve God acceptably. You may be religious and humble yourself, going through the motions, but you'll never have the true joy, relationship, or peace that God intended for you to have because you'll be living with sin-consciousness.

Once Was Enough

Hebrews 9:15 begins with the phrase *"for this cause."* For what cause? For the cause of Jesus purging your conscience from dead works, because your conscience can now be reset, cleansed, and purged to where it doesn't condemn you but instead gives you confidence and boldness. Very few Christians live in this place, but this is what Hebrews 9:15 is all about: *"For this cause he is the mediator of the new testament, that by means of death, for the redemption of the transgressions that were under the first testament, they which are called might receive the promise of eternal inheritance."*

Hebrews 9:12, which I opened this chapter with, talks about eternal redemption, and Hebrews 9:15 talks about eternal inheritance. Many in the body of Christ believe you lose your inheritance every time you sin, and if you die with unconfessed sin in your life you'll go to hell, even if you've been walking with the Lord for decades. This is completely contrary to everything the New Covenant stands for and represents.

This was the case under the Old Covenant, however. If a person died with unconfessed sin—a sin that hadn't been atoned for—they'd lose everything, even though they had been walking with God for a long time. The Lord would leave the person and separate from them. But under the New Covenant, He'll never leave us nor forsake us (Heb. 13:5).

Every time your conscience condemns you with, "You messed up again, you sorry thing. What makes you think God can answer your prayer and love you? What makes you think God could use you?" you have to purge your conscience with the truths found in Hebrews 9. Verses 12, 14, 15, 26, and 28 prove that Jesus has set you free, perfected you, and cleansed you forever. You cannot lose your right standing with God.

> ***For Christ is not entered into the holy places made with hands, which are the figures of the true; but into heaven itself, now to appear in the presence of God for us: nor yet that he should offer himself often, as the high priest entereth into the holy place***

every year with blood of others; for then must he often have suffered since the foundation of the world: but now once in the end of the world hath he appeared to put away sin by the sacrifice of himself.

Hebrews 9:24-26

If Jesus was still doing things the way they were done in the Old Testament, He would have to offer Himself over and over and over. If you always have to put your sins under the blood, Jesus would have to be dying and shedding His blood and reapplying His blood constantly. Jesus couldn't sit at the right hand of God (Heb. 10:12) if He had to offer a new sacrifice and make atonement for us every time we sinned. He only had to do it once.

Hebrews 9:26 is saying that Jesus is not doing things the same way they were done under the Old Covenant. His one-time sacrifice perfected us forever. Again, in verses 27-28, we see that Jesus, with one sacrifice, has paid for all of our sins, even those we haven't yet committed:

And as it is appointed unto men once to die, but after this the judgment: so Christ was once offered to bear the sins of many; and unto them that look for him shall he appear the second time without sin unto salvation.

Look also at Hebrews 10:10-12:

We are sanctified through the offering of the body of Jesus Christ once for all. And every priest standeth daily ministering and offering oftentimes the same sacrifices, which can never take away sins: But this man, after he had offered one sacrifice for sins for ever, sat down on the right hand of God."

Jesus offered one sacrifice not just for all people but for all time. If you use the verses I've discussed so far in this chapter when your conscience tries to condemn you, you will purge your conscience from dead works. Then you can be empowered to serve God and resist the devil, and he will flee from you (James 4:7).

You Are Perfect!

Many people have a problem with Hebrews 10:14, which reads, *"For by one offering he hath perfected for ever them that are sanctified."* As we just read in Hebrews 10:10, we have been sanctified *"once for all."* And, if we're sanctified, we are now perfected (verse 14). Some people struggle and ask, "What do you mean I'm perfected?" after they look in the mirror and see zits, gray hairs, and wrinkles. Then they search their soulish realm and discover all sorts of fears and dysfunctions.

Hebrews 10:14 isn't talking about our body or soul. Our spirit is what gets born again, and our spirit is what becomes sanctified and perfected forever. Hebrews 12:22-23 explains this further:

> *But ye are come unto mount Sion, and unto the city of the living God, the heavenly Jerusalem, and to an innumerable company of angels, to the general assembly and church of the firstborn, which are written in heaven, and to God the Judge of all, and to the spirits of just men made perfect.*

Our physical body will eventually change; and according to 1 Corinthians 13:9-12, our soulish realm will also change because

right now we only know in part, but someday we'll know all things. But our spirit is sanctified and perfected forever. Ephesians 4:24 tells us that our new man is *"created in righteousness and true holiness."* The moment we are saved, we are *"sealed with that holy Spirit of promise"* (Eph. 1:13); our spirit is vacuum packed!

As Christians, when we sin, that sin could afflict our physical body with sickness and our natural lives with poverty and so forth, or it could affect our soul by causing condemnation and giving Satan an inroad into our life. But that sin cannot penetrate the seal around our spirit. Our spirit retains its righteousness and holiness.

God is a Spirit, and He sees us in the spirit realm (John 4:24). Even though we may be a mess in the natural, when we approach God in Jesus's name, we instantly enter into the holy of holies in our spirit, which has been sanctified and perfected forever (Heb. 10:14). This is how we can still fellowship and relate to God even though we sin.

These truths will change your life and how you relate to God. It is so awesome to know that Jesus's one sacrifice has paid the price for all of our sins—past, present, and future. And because of His death, our spirit is sanctified, and God now sees us just as He sees Jesus—we are perfect in His sight! It is good news to know that we no longer have to live with a consciousness of sin, but our conscience can be purged so that we are free to serve the living God. Praise God!

CHAPTER 12

Go and Sin No More

If you understand and receive the truths in chapters 9 and 10 of Hebrews, you will be able to purge your conscience from dead works. And knowing that you have been sanctified and perfected forever will completely set you free to serve the Lord. While this is awesome news, there is a balance to it. The balance is that we can't use God's grace and forgiveness of sin as a license to go and sin some more.

Some people will want to take what I've been teaching here and say, "I love this! I can go live in sin now. I've been sanctified and perfected forever." To these people, I'll say, "You need to get born again." Anyone who thinks this way is not truly saved. I can say that because of 1 John 3:1-3:

> *Behold, what manner of love the Father hath bestowed upon us, that we should be called the sons of God: therefore the world*

> ***knoweth us not, because it knew him not. Beloved, now are we the sons of God, and it doth not yet appear what we shall be: but we know that, when he shall appear, we shall be like him; for we shall see him as he is. And every man that hath this hope in him purifieth himself, even as he is pure.***

If you're truly born again, you want to purify yourself. You may be doing a poor job of it because the Law actually makes sin come alive in us and ultimately hurts us by causing us to lust for the very thing we were told we can't have. But if you were truly born again, you would hate the fact that you're letting sin dominate you. And you definitely wouldn't be looking for an excuse to live in sin.

God's grace won't set you free *to* sin; it will set you free *from* sin. It will give you power over sin: *"For sin shall not have dominion over you: for ye are not under the law, but under grace"* (Rom. 6:14). The Law binds you to sin and gives sin dominion over you. Grace breaks the dominion of sin.

Jesus has made atonement for your sins, paying for all of your sins—past, present, and future—through one sacrifice, so you can now live without any sin-consciousness. If you learn this and then use it as an excuse to sin, you were never born again in the first place. If you truly love God, you won't look for an excuse to sin. You'll want to break free from sin.

You're as Holy as Jesus

Many people today profess Christianity, but they don't possess it. They don't have a real relationship with the Lord. These people will go to church to pay God their dues, hoping that somehow or another He'll be pleased with them. They've never had a true born-again experience, so if they hear a message of forgiveness and grace like this, they might use it as an excuse to live in sin because they never knew the Lord in the first place.

On the other hand, if you're truly born again, this message will make you fall in love with God. You'll want to discover how much He loves you, realizing that even with all the rotten stuff you've done, you can still approach God as if you've never sinned.

This is my layman's definition of the word *justified:* "just as if I'd never sinned." When God looks at me, He doesn't see my old self, and He doesn't see my sin. Even when I still mess up and blow it, he's looking at me in the spirit. And in the spirit, I'm perfect, I'm his workmanship, I'm righteous, I'm pure, I'm sanctified, and I'm perfected forever.

People who are under the Law may believe that God will let them into heaven, but there are so many Christians who limp through life bearing the sin and unworthiness of their past life. They're going to live their entire Christian life feeling like second-class Christians, somehow inferior to others because of their sin.

But all they have to do is purge their conscience from those evil works through the blood of Jesus. Then they can reach a place where they are no longer conscious of sin. Under the New Covenant, it's not a fear of rejection, shame, or unworthiness that drives people to God but love—love for His tremendous sacrifice. And there is no fear in love:

> *There is no fear in love; but perfect love casteth out fear: because fear hath torment. He that feareth is not made perfect in love.*
>
> **1 John 4:18**

There shouldn't be any fear in God's perfect love, yet the average Christian lives with a lot of fear, along with feelings of unworthiness. This is not how God wants us to relate to Him. The Lord has forgiven you more than you can ever understand. We struggle with this because we don't have a role model for it. Nobody in the natural treats us as good as God treats us. You may have people who are decent or polite to you, but if you do something really wrong, they won't want you to be close to them again.

God's not like that. He doesn't just tolerate you. He makes you a brand-new person who is as clean and pure as He is (Eph. 4:24). According to 1 John 4:17, in your spirit you're as righteous and holy as Jesus.

> *Herein is our love made perfect, that we may have boldness in the day of judgment: because as he is, so are we in this world.*

This doesn't say "so are we going to be in the future world." It says, "*so are we in this world.*" This isn't true of your physical body or your actions. At your very best, you still aren't as good as He is. It's also not true in your soulish realm. At your very best, your soulish realm has still fallen short of who God is. But in your spirit you are identical to Jesus. You are as pure and holy as Jesus because He created you that way. He sanctified you and perfected you forever, so you can come before God with no more conscience of sin.

Thank God for His Goodness

The average religious person today comes before the Lord saying, "Oh Lord, I come before You so humbly today. I'm so unworthy. I don't deserve anything." That's the way we've been taught to enter into God's presence.

God has a different way for us to enter His presence:

> *Enter into his gates with thanksgiving, and into his courts with praise: be thankful unto him, and bless his name. For the LORD is good; and his mercy is everlasting; and his truth endureth to all generations.*
>
> **Psalm 100:4-5**

Instead of entering God's presence reciting all of our unworthiness—which is in the flesh, not in the spirit—we ought to come in the spirit and start praising him: "Father, thank You that I'm holy and pure." If you've done something wrong, and you recognize your sin, that should amplify the goodness of God even more. Tell God, "I messed up so badly. I embarrassed myself and You. I'm a mess, but in the spirit, I'm still righteous and holy and pure, and You love me." That ought to make you praise Him that much more.

If you have lived a terrible life, and if people don't even know half of what you've done, you ought to be more excited about being righteous and holy than anyone else. You're as holy and pure as Jesus! I don't care how rotten you've been, how vile you've been, or how debased you've been. When you make Jesus your Lord, you are as pure as snow. You are righteous and holy and pure. And you ought to praise and thank God for that instead of feeling like you're a second-class citizen.

If we understood everything that Jesus has done for us, we would be completely overwhelmed. Jesus has been better to us than we deserve or understand. If somehow or another I could imagine being God, and if I loved people enough to die for them, it would break my heart to think that these people I died for are never going to know how good I've been to them.

They think that I've forgiven them to the degree that maybe I'll let them into heaven, but for whatever reason, I'm still upset with them. I won't answer their prayers, they won't be blessed, and I won't use them because of their sin. If I had done all of this, sacrificed everything for them, and they didn't appreciate it, that would be tragic. But that's exactly how some people act toward God.

We have to get the revelation that when we became born again, all of our sin had already been dealt with. Many people are afraid that if they truly receive all God has done for them and embrace grace, they would start living for the devil. They wouldn't, because if they ever walked in God's love so much that they could purge their conscience completely so they had no more conscience of sin, they'd be living holier accidentally than they ever had on purpose before.

God foresaw everything we would ever do, and He forgave us of all past, present, and even future sin. Understanding this doesn't free us *to* sin, but it frees us *from* sin.

In the next chapter, we'll take a look at why, even though we've been forgiven of our sins, there are still consequences to sin. And we'll discover what steps Christians should take if they yield themselves to sin.

CHAPTER 13

God Doesn't Have a Problem with Your Sin

We learned earlier from Hebrews 10:22 that we need to sprinkle our hearts with the blood of Jesus in order to be set free from an evil conscience because our conscience is not a perfect standard. Again, all our conscience does is tell us whether we're right or wrong. It will never tell us that we're forgiven. It never says that God loves us in spite of the things we've done. It's been programmed to show us our failures.

Imagine what it would be like if you had a friend who constantly did nothing but point out everything you did wrong. This friend never complimented or encouraged you. I guarantee that you wouldn't be friends with that person for long. This is exactly what your conscience does. It tells you when you're wrong.

It's constantly pulling an inventory, letting you know what you could've done better.

I have never preached a message in my life where I felt like it was just awesome. Every time I preach, I think I could've done a better job. Recently, one of our Charis Bible College students preached a message that was really good. Afterward, this student started pointing out all the things that could've been better about the message. His conscience was condemning him. In response, I said, "I've never preached a message where I said everything that I wanted to say. You just do the best you can and then let it go."

If you aren't careful, you'll become a perfectionist who nitpicks and criticizes everything. Some of you don't even have to have an enemy do this for you. You do it to yourselves. Your conscience is alive and well, constantly condemning you and showing you what you could've done better. If you don't sprinkle your heart from an evil conscience, according to Hebrews 10:22, you'll never really enjoy the kind of relationship with God that He wants you to have.

The kind of relationship God wants us to have with Him is based on Hebrews 8:10-11, which tells us how God has given us a new heart under the New Covenant:

> *For this is the covenant that I will make with the house of Israel after those days, saith the Lord; I will put my laws into their mind, and write them in their hearts: and I will be to them a God, and they shall be to me a people: And they shall not teach every man his neighbor, and every man his*

> ***brother, saying, Know the Lord: for all shall know me, from the least to the greatest.***

These verses have been interpreted by many to say that every Jew will be born again, but that's not what this passage is talking about. This means that every person who receives this New Covenant will be taught directly from the Lord. You won't have to take somebody else's word for what God is saying. You can have a personal relationship with the Lord. He will speak to you personally. Each one of us who receives salvation will have a personal relationship with God.

Continuing in verse 12, God says, *"For I will be merciful to their unrighteousness, and their sins and their iniquities will I remember no more."* Part of this New Covenant relationship is that God will no longer hold our sins against us. This is contrary to what 99.9 percent of Christianity believes today. Christianity preaches that God is angry with you, He's going to judge you, He's going to punish you, and He won't bless you. Some even preach that you might lose your salvation if you sin, or at the very least, God will no longer fellowship with you or use you. After all, they argue, God won't use a dirty vessel. I've got news for you: God doesn't have any other kind of vessel to use!

Hebrews 10:17-18 is a similar passage, which states:

> ***And their sins and iniquities will I remember no more. Now where remission of these is, there is no more offering for sin.***

This is an awesome passage! Most Christians believe that every time they sin they have to plead for God to apply His blood to them because they have to get their sin under the blood. But, as I've talked about before, our sins have already been forgiven—past, present, and future. We have obtained eternal redemption (Heb. 9:22).

What about 1 John 1:9?

Now, I know that when some people hear this, they think of 1 John 1:9, where the apostle John said, *"If we confess our sins, he is faithful and just to forgive us our sins, and to cleanse us from all unrighteousness."* It clearly says here that we have to confess our sins. So, how do we reconcile this?

So far, I've offered several scriptures within just two chapters of Hebrews stating that we've been sanctified and perfected forever and that we have eternal redemption and eternal inheritance. How do we harmonize these verses with 1 John 1:9? I touched on this some in chapter 11, but the key is realizing that our spirit is the part of us that is born again. This is the part of us that was changed when we received salvation and is now sealed by the Holy Spirit (Eph. 1:13). When we sin as Christians, sin enters into our bodies. Sin gives Satan access to us, but it doesn't touch our born-again spirits.

I've talked with people who have lung problems, throat problems, and other issues as a result of smoking, and they're still smoking. They've wanted me to pray for them, and I've told them, "God loves you and wants you well, but you are giving Satan direct access to your body, and there are consequences." When a person continues to smoke but then prays for God's healing, it is like chasing the devil out the back door but leaving the front door wide open. You have to close the door on that sin.

If you live in sin, it gives Satan an inroad into your physical body as well as your mind and emotions (the soulish realm). But your spirit remains sealed by the Holy Spirit (Eph. 1:13). Your sin cannot penetrate this seal. Your spirit remains righteous, holy, pure, and clean. It is not defiled by your sin.

But does that mean that you just keep sinning? If you do, you are doing so to your own detriment because you're giving Satan a free shot at you in the physical and soulish realms. You're foolish to ever let the devil have free access to your soul and body and then think that you'll prosper (John 10:10). You can say, "Well, God loves me. I'm forgiven of all sin. That's what Andrew Wommack said, and so I'm going to go out and rob a bank because God has already forgiven me."

God has forgiven you, and the whole time you're sitting in your jail cell, He will be right there with you. He'll fellowship with you and tell you that He loves you, and in spite of what you've done, He still thinks you're awesome. You can have a wonderful time with God as you sit in jail! There are consequences to your sin, and you're foolish if you continue to live in sin.

So, let's say that a Christian acts foolishly and yields themselves to sin. How do you deal with that? That person's sin is already forgiven. Their spirit is already purged. Do they just forget it and ignore it? No. That's what 1 John 1:9 is about. That sin needs to be confessed.

The word *confess* here basically means to say the same thing or to agree. In other words, God said, "Go this way," and you said, "I don't think so. I think I'm going to go this way." You think your way is better than God's, so you get over on the wrong path and then you crash and burn. Nothing's working, people are mad at you, you end up in jail or whatever, and all of a sudden you finally say, "God, I agree with You. You were right. Your way was better."

The moment you humble yourself and confess your sin, the forgiveness that's already a reality in your spirit comes out into your soul and into your body, and Satan no longer has rights to you because you've humbled yourself before the Lord.

First Peter 5:6 tells us,

> *Humble yourselves therefore under the mighty hand of God, that he may exalt you in due time.*

James 4:10 tells us,

> *Humble yourselves in the sight of the Lord, and he shall lift you up.*

You Can't Have It Both Ways

It's still important to confess your sin, but not for the purpose of having it forgiven, as if it is for your eternal salvation. Those scriptures that I've already used illustrate that we've been forgiven of our sins—past, present, and future. Our spirit is secure in Christ. But when we yield ourselves to the devil through sin, he will eat our lunch and pop the bag!

> ***Know ye not, that to whom ye yield yourselves servants to obey, his servants ye are to whom ye obey; whether of sin unto death, or of obedience unto righteousness?***
>
> **Romans 6:16**

So, what do you do? If you've given place to the devil through sin, you confess it. You humble yourself. When you do, your body and soul will come under the dominion of God, and Satan will no longer have access to you. But a person who continues in sin is like a person who beats their hand with a hammer, all the while saying, "God, please take away the pain." *Bam, bam, bam!* "God, take away the pain." Yet that person just can't understand why they still have pain. How dumb can you get and still breathe? Quit hitting yourself. Just quit sinning! Quit giving Satan access to your life.

Satan has a legal right to you when you yield yourself to him through sin. You gave him control and permission. How do you stop that? By confessing that sin. This doesn't affect your spirit man. It doesn't affect your eternal destiny. Your spirit has been sanctified and perfected forever. It has been sealed by the Holy Spirit, and there is no impurity that can get into your spirit.

John 4:24 tells us that God is a Spirit. He still sees you in the spirit and still sees you as righteous, holy, and pure, even though you have just defiled yourself and given Satan an inroad into your life. God still loves you and is not mad at you. He's already forgiven you, but you need to quit giving Satan a free shot at you.

> ***The thief cometh not, but for to steal, and to kill, and to destroy: I am come that they might have life, and that they might have it more abundantly.***
>
> **John 10:10**

Satan is out to destroy you, and if you yield to him through sin, he *will*. Don't do it. I deal with the conflict of sin in people all the time. People tell me they want prayer, and I know God wants them well. He loves them and wants to set them free, but there are reasons why they're in the mess they're in. I don't always know what those reasons are, but sometimes it's obvious that they aren't cooperating with God. They aren't seeking God; they're just out there living a life completely contrary to what the Word of God says, yet they want the results that come through living a holy life and cooperating and walking with God.

It's a problem because God wants you to have all His benefits, but you can't live one way and experience God's blessings at the same time. It's not because God doesn't want to bless you and give things to you. It's because you're giving Satan free access to your life. First John 1:9 has nothing to do with your eternal salvation, but it's simply that when you recognize that you've given place to the devil, you stop his entrance into your life through repentance and confession.

Not a Big Deal

First John 1:9 is the only scripture I'm aware of in the New Testament that tells a Christian to confess sin and receive forgiveness. James 5:15-16 mentions that if you've *"committed sins"* to *"confess your faults one to another, and pray one for another."* These verses talk about humbling ourselves and telling each other about our faults, but they don't talk about confessing our sins to God, as 1 John 1:9 does.

My point here is that if this was as big of a deal as the church has made it out to be—where you have to get your sins confessed and put them under the blood so that God will forgive you and fellowship with you—then there would certainly be more than one mention of it in the New Testament (Matt. 18:16 and 2 Cor. 13:1). You often hear people say that you have to confess your sins and ask God to forgive you and come into your heart. That's not what the Scriptures teach.

In Acts 16, when God rescued Paul and Silas from prison, the alarmed Philippian jailer asked Paul and Silas how to receive salvation:

> [The jailer] *brought* [Paul and Silas] *out, and said, Sirs, what must I do to be saved? And they said, Believe on the Lord Jesus Christ, and thou shalt be saved, and thy house.*
>
> Acts 16:30-31, brackets added

Paul and Silas didn't tell the man to confess his sins, only to believe on the Lord. Salvation isn't dependent on you confessing all your sins. What would happen to you if you forgot one of your sins? Does that mean it's not covered? You don't have to confess your sins for salvation. You just have to confess your faith in Jesus for the forgiveness of your sins. This is what salvation is about. When you sin, you're not separated from God again until you ask Him to forgive you of that sin. Hebrews 10:18 says, *"Now where remission of these is, there is no more offering for sins."*

Jesus's one sacrifice has dealt with your sin forever. He has atoned for all of your sins. Sin is no longer the issue with God. Most Christians believe that sin is a problem. I agree that it is. But the question is, "Why is it a problem?" Most Christians believe it's a problem because it breaks your fellowship with God. They believe He won't answer your prayers, He won't move on your behalf, He won't use you, and He won't bless you. I'm telling you that sin is a nonissue with God.

Sin Is Deadly

Sin is, however, a big issue with the devil and with people. If you start sinning against people by criticizing them, saying hurtful things, or lying, you're going to have trouble in your relationships. Sin causes problems.

Sin has consequences among people, and it's a direct path for Satan to get into your life. It's true that sin hinders us. According to James 1:15, sin is deadly: *"sin, when it is finished, bringeth forth death."*

Sin will take you further than you want to go, keep you longer than you want to stay, and cost you more than you want to pay. Satan is going to hurt you through sickness, disease, poverty, and relationships. The church has seen that sin causes problems, but people just assume that it's God who is causing the problems. But it's not God.

God does not withdraw from you because of sin. If He did, which sins would cause Him to withdraw? You'd have to categorize them, with the rationale that there are big sins, but then there are others you can get away with. Romans 14:23 tells us that *"whatsoever is not of faith is sin."* If you're going to use the Bible to define sin, God would never have anything to do with any of us because we all fall short (Rom. 3:23).

God is not mad at you. He's not even in a bad mood. He's never going to be mad at you. God loves you, and that's it. He loves you, period, and there's nothing you can do about it. You can't make God love you any *more*, and you can't make God love you any less. Once you become born again, He will never leave you nor forsake you (Heb. 13:5). He will never withdraw from you. He will constantly hear your prayers.

But there's a lot you can do to make *you* love God less. There's a lot you can do that will harden your heart and blind you and deaden you, making you insensitive toward Him. Every time you sin and every time you violate your conscience, you put a layer of insensitivity between you and God. If you live that way long enough, you can become spiritually dull and non-perceptive. You will no longer hear from God, and you'll assume God's not speaking to you because you're living in sin. No, God's still speaking. You just can't hear. You've become deaf because of your sin.

Some people may say, "What's the difference whether it's God or the devil or whatever?" It's a huge difference! It's a huge difference for God to be mad at you and withhold things from you versus you giving place to the devil. The bottom line to all this is that if you're living in sin, you're not prospering. So, do not live in sin. I repeat: do not live in sin!

CHAPTER 14

Be Bold

Having therefore, brethren, boldness to enter into the holiest by the blood of Jesus.

Hebrews 10:19

Did you know that when these words were written, they would've been considered blasphemy to the religious Jews? No one could enter into the holy of holies except the high priest once a year, and then only under certain conditions. This verse says that we have boldness to enter into the very presence of God—into the holy of holies. This was offensive to the Jews because they were constantly separated from God because of their sin and their conscience that couldn't be purged.

But now, in the New Covenant, we should *"have no more conscience of sins"* (Heb. 10:2). Jesus has already dealt with all of our sin, so we ought to have boldness to enter into God's presence without fearing His rejection and punishment. We don't have to come crawling into His presence as if He were going to beat us.

I grew up in Arlington, Texas, during the "Jesus Movement" in the hippie days and was raised in a Baptist church. One thing I was taught was that I was a sinner. I knew that I had *"sinned, and come short of the glory of God"* (Rom. 3:23), and I was really, really, really aware of my sinfulness. Well, one night I went to a Bible study, and a woman was leading the study. I was offended right away by the fact that a woman was teaching. That wasn't an acceptable Baptist practice. In the Baptist church, women could teach children, but they couldn't teach a male adult.

But I just decided to be gracious, so I sat there and "put up with" her teaching until a longhaired hippie proclaimed that he was the righteousness of God. I just couldn't tolerate that at all! In my church, if your hair touched your collar you went directly to hell. So, when this longhaired hippie—who smelled bad, by the way—stood up and said he was the righteousness of God, I had all I could take. I stood up too, and used my three scriptures on him: *"All have sinned, and come short of the glory of God"* (Rom. 3:23); *"There is none righteous, no, not one"* (Rom. 3:10); and *"all our righteousnesses are as filthy rags"* (Is. 64:6), and I just blasted him.

I was prepared for an onslaught of an attack against me, but instead this guy was kind to me and loved on me. For every one scripture I quoted, he quoted ten scriptures back to me about how he was righteous. It didn't convince me, but it shocked me. I thought, *Well, God, I didn't represent You very well.* After that I bought a *Young's Analytical Concordance* and looked up every instance of the words *righteous* and *righteousness* in the entire Bible. There are hundreds of them. And that was back before we had computers, so I wrote them all out on a legal pad. I wrote down every scripture in the Bible on righteousness; then I categorized them so I could understand them better.

Then I fasted and prayed for a whole week and spent fifteen hours a day studying this out. By the end of the week, I was completely convinced that I was righteous, not because I deserved it but because the Word said so. At the end of Romans 5, it says five different times that in the same way that we were born sinners, we were also born again righteous.

I had accepted the fact that I was born a sinner, but I hadn't accepted that I was born again righteous, and I certainly didn't feel righteous. It was contrary to everything I'd been taught. But I just had to bow my knee to the Word and admit that I didn't understand it, but according to the Bible I was righteous.

> ***But of him are ye in Christ Jesus, who of God is made unto us wisdom, and righteousness, and sanctification, and redemption.***
>
> **1 Corinthians 1:30**

No More Whining!

This was just soaking in, and I wasn't overjoyed about it. I was bothered because this went against everything I'd been taught. I was reeling with this in my mind. I remember going out to my back porch to sit down and just think about it. I had a dog that I gotten for my mother to be a watchdog when I went into the army. It was three-fourths German shepherd and one-fourth chow. It was a huge dog that looked really mean and had a bad bark. But if you opened the gate and walked into the backyard, it would hurt itself getting out of the way. Someone had once beaten that dog with a trace chain. Because of that, the dog would run across the yard and get about five or six feet from me, roll over on its side, and then scoot up to me whimpering and whining like I was going to beat it.

I had named the dog Honey because she had a honey-colored coat. I'd had her for years, and she still acted like that. So, as I was meditating on being the righteousness of God, I told the Lord that I just couldn't understand it. And while I was sitting there, here came Honey. She came running toward me and then scooted down like she always did. I just lost it! I said, "Honey, one time I would like for you to jump on me like a normal dog and not act like I'm going to beat you. Everyone who sees you thinks I'm just terrible to you. You act like I treat you horribly."

As I continued to read my dog the riot act, God spoke to me, saying, "That's the way I feel about you. Every time you come to Me, it's 'Oh God, I'm so unworthy. I come before You so humbly. Oh God, I don't deserve anything.'" He continued, "You just get on your side and whimper and whine, and one time I'd like for you to come boldly to My throne of grace and act like I've forgiven you."

Man, was that ever a turning point in my life! And that's what Hebrews 10:19-20 is talking about:

> *Having therefore, brethren, boldness to enter into the holiest by the blood of Jesus. By a new and living way, which he hath consecrated for us, through the veil, that is to say, his flesh.*

Every word used here is important. Verse 20 says, *"By a new and living way."* Most Christians are still approaching God the same way an Old Testament saint did, hoping that He will forgive them, instead of understanding that He has *already* forgiven them. Instead of basking in the love and forgiveness that we already have, we come to God every time we sin and ask, "God, will You please forgive me? God, could You please use me?"

Every time you approach God like this, it's dishonoring what Jesus has done. You aren't esteeming what He did for you. You're acting like you still have to pay for your sin. As a matter of fact, there are many people who ask God for forgiveness, and then they suffer for a certain period of time until they feel like they've atoned for their sin. Once they've suffered enough, they believe that they can then come back into God's presence. That's not

taking advantage of what Jesus did. That's approaching God on your own righteousness.

Many of you, if you messed up and sinned, feel that you have to do without the joy and presence of the Lord for a certain period of time to atone for yourself. This is really no different than what some Catholics in South America do, where they beat themselves and crawl over broken glass during Lent to atone for their sin. That's wrong. You don't have to do that. Jesus has already atoned for your sin. You don't have to punish yourself. Yet most of us feel that we have to suffer. We can't bask in the joy of the Lord.

If you sin, it honors God for you to say, "God, I am such a mess. I've sinned again, but I know that You still love me, and I'm going to come boldly into Your presence, not because I deserve it, but because I put my faith in Jesus. I honor You, and I'm standing on Your atonement." It would bless God for you to do that.

Jumping onto God's Lap

Hebrews 10:20 says that now we have a new way. In chapter 10, I taught on how there is a difference between the Old Covenant way of approaching God and the New Covenant way. The New Covenant way is a *"living way, which he hath consecrated for us, through the veil, that is to say, his flesh."* This makes it very clear that the Old Testament veil that separated the holy place from the holy of holies where God dwelt was symbolic of the flesh of Jesus.

No one can approach God except through Jesus:

I am the way, the truth, and the life: no man cometh unto the Father, but by me.

John 14:6

The Old Testament veil separated us from the presence of God. But when Jesus died, that veil was torn in two from top to bottom (Matt. 27:51). In Herod's temple, the veil was over sixty feet tall, very thick, and had gold thread woven throughout the curtain. Josephus wrote that you couldn't tie a team of horses to that veil and tear it. It was so heavy and so thick, there was no way it could be torn. If somehow or another this sixty-foot veil could've been torn in two, you wouldn't have been able to get enough leverage to tear it from the top. It had to have been God who tore it. God rent this veil, and it was symbolic of Jesus and how the way between us and the very presence of God is no longer blocked.

We can now come directly into God's presence and approach Him as our Abba Father. *Abba* is an affectionate term meaning "Daddy God." Having the veil torn in two creates an image of how we can walk into God's presence and jump up on His lap. That doesn't mean we're irreverent, but we can act like His children when we're with Him.

If I was at your house and your child walked into the kitchen and said, "I know I don't deserve anything. I didn't make my bed today. I haven't made the best grades in school. I know I'm not doing everything I could, but can I please, please, please have something to eat? I may not deserve a whole meal, but could you just give me a little?" If that child continued to beg for food like that, I'd think that something was definitely wrong with the relationship you had with your child.

Obviously, your children should honor you and respect you, but there's nothing wrong with a kid coming to you and saying, "I'm hungry. I want something to eat." Parents actually like that. They like that familiarity. They like that their children will draw on the relationship they have with them without any fear.

Religion has taught us that we have to come to God acting like we're unworthy and undeserving. We just beg God for crumbs because we're so unworthy. If this is you, then you aren't approaching God in a New Covenant manner. You're acting like the veil is still up, and there is still a separation between you and God. That behavior is evidence that your conscience has not been purged by the blood of the Lord Jesus.

Full Assurance

Hebrews 10:21-22 continues, *"And having an high priest over the house of God; Let us draw near with a true heart in full assurance of faith."* This is saying that you can have faith, and then you can be assured of your faith, but you can also have full assurance of faith. There are varying degrees of faith, trust, and reliance upon God and what Jesus did on the cross.

We're supposed to have *"full assurance of faith, having our hearts sprinkled from an evil conscience, and our bodies washed with pure water"* (Heb. 10:22). You cannot come before God confidently if you haven't cleansed your conscience. And this is how many Christians live. They live with a defiled conscience and sin-consciousness. They aren't cleansed *"from dead works to serve the living God"* (Heb. 9:14), and their own heart condemns them.

This is not theoretical. I pray with thousands and thousands of people. I can guarantee you that the vast majority of these people do not doubt that God has the power to change their situation. That's the reason they ask me to pray. They believe that God can heal them or provide whatever they need. But they aren't confident. They don't have the confidence to believe that God will answer *their* prayer because they have a defiled conscience. They think they have to have someone else, like me, pray. They believe that somehow or another I'm holier than they are. If they knew me as well as they know themselves, they wouldn't have any more faith in my prayers than they have in theirs.

We tend to think that ministers have it all together, but I don't have it all together. All my righteousness comes from Jesus, and I have to purge my conscience and not try to receive God's power based on my goodness. I tell people how I've seen people raised from the dead, including my own son and my wife. I've seen a lot of miracles happen, and most people I minister to believe that God still works miracles. People who believe in this don't doubt that I've seen people raised from the dead.

There are others, however, who say that this type of thing doesn't happen. I've been kicked off television and radio stations because they heard me say that I've seen people raised from the dead, and they've called me a liar. They don't believe God works miracles today, so they kicked me off their station for saying so. But since you're reading this book, you're probably a fanatic, or a fanatic you know gave it to you to read.

So, you probably believe in God's miracles. And if you came to one of my meetings and someone fell over dead, and I said we were going to raise that person from the dead, you would be in agreement with me. In fact, you'd probably come up close and want to see it. But if I said, "If you believe God still performs miracles, *you* come pray for this person to be raised from the dead," suddenly your faith would turn to fear. Your excitement would turn to dread. You wouldn't be nearly as excited about it if you were the one praying.

Shipwrecked Faith

What happened? What changed? Did God change? Did God all of a sudden stop doing miracles? The reason you wouldn't have confidence is because most of us have God's power and ability tied to our own performance. You know you, and you know you don't deserve it. Your conscience condemns you, and your faith becomes shipwrecked.

> *This charge I commit unto thee, son Timothy, according to the prophecies which went before on thee, that thou by them mightest war a good warfare; holding faith, and a good conscience; which some having put away concerning faith have made shipwreck.*
>
> **1 Timothy 1:18-19**

In these verses, Paul is telling Timothy that you have to fight, and prophecy is one of the things that allows us to fight and wage a good warfare. Verse 18 says that we are in a battle; we are fighting. I guarantee that Satan is out to destroy people, and he will seek the precious life. The more in leadership you are and the more you grow in the Lord, the more the devil's going to target you.

This is not a bad thing because you will still be equipped to walk in victory. I'm not saying that you won't be victorious and that you won't win. But to think that somehow or another you grow beyond Satan fighting you is not what Scripture teaches. We are in a warfare, and you fight by *"holding faith, and a good conscience."* If your conscience isn't clear, or if your conscience is condemning you, it will make your faith shipwrecked.

Shipwrecked means that you left port, you moved in the right direction, but you never arrived. This perfectly describes the lives of many Christians. Most Christians are believing God, and they may see some success. But as far as seeing the fulfillment of their faith and the conclusion of where everything's working, the average Christian is not experiencing that kind of victory.

There may be a lot of reasons why this is so, but one reason is that not having your conscience purged from evil can cause your faith to be shipwrecked. People ask God why He isn't answering their prayers, but it's not God who isn't answering. The problem is that we aren't receiving because our own conscience condemns us and drives us away. In John 8:9, Jesus wrote on the sand when the adulterous woman was being stoned, and Scripture says that the crowd *"being convicted by their own conscience, went out one by one."*

Did you know that a clear conscience is not something that happens automatically? After we're *"sprinkled from an evil conscience"* (Heb. 10:2), we have to take the Word of God, apply it to our life, and encourage ourselves in the Lord. In the next chapter, we'll look at some practical examples of how to do this.

CHAPTER 15

It's Time to Encourage Yourself!

And it came to pass, when David and his men were come to Ziklag on the third day, that the Amalekites had invaded the south, and Ziklag, and smitten Ziklag, and burned it with fire; and had taken the women captives, that were therein: they slew not any, either great or small, but carried them away, and went on their way. So David and his men came to the city, and, behold, it was burned with fire; and their wives, and their sons, and their daughters, were taken captives. Then David and the people that were with him lifted up their voice and wept, until they had no more power to weep. And David's two wives were taken captives, Ahinoam the Jezreelitess, and Abigail the wife of Nabal the Carmelite. And David was greatly distressed; for

> ***the people spake of stoning him, because the soul of all the people was grieved, every man for his sons and for his daughters: but David encouraged himself in the LORD his God. And David said to Abiathar the priest, Ahimelech's son, I pray thee, bring me hither the ephod. And Abiathar brought thither the ephod to David. And David enquired at the LORD, saying, Shall I pursue after this troop? shall I overtake them? And he answered him, Pursue: for thou shalt surely overtake them, and without fail recover all.***
>
> **1 Samuel 30:1-8**

David had been anointed to be king for over thirteen years, and he had spent much of this time running from his father-in-law, Saul, who wanted to kill him. A lot of bad things happened to David, but he finally returned to his hometown of Ziklag. We see in this passage that the Amalekites had invaded the town and burned down all of their homes. Then they took the wives and children of the town captive and fled with them. When David and his men returned home, they saw that their entire city was destroyed. They *"wept, until they had no more power to weep"* (1 Sam. 30:4).

David suffered thirteen years. A series of terrible things had happened ever since he was anointed by God to be king. His own men even spoke of stoning him to death. This would've been a great opportunity for him to just quit. I'm certain he was facing more adversity than any of us have ever faced. It was really bad for David, yet verse 6 says that he *"encouraged himself in the LORD his God."*

To encourage himself, he called for the ephod, which was the way a person inquired of God. He called for the Word of God and began to encourage himself. You know what he was doing? He was dealing with his conscience. It looked like nothing was working out for David. He was ready to quit, and he was down and discouraged.

We learned earlier that when Adam and Eve gained a conscience, they suddenly became full of shame (Gen. 3:7-10). They became fearful and hid from God. All of those things are byproducts of the conscience. David was discouraged, so he began to build himself up and encourage himself in the Lord. He didn't wait for someone else to encourage him.

David didn't have what we have today; he didn't have salvation the way we have it. He wasn't forgiven of all of his past, present, and future sins. He also didn't have the Holy Spirit the way that we do. The Holy Spirit could come and go upon David, but today the Holy Spirit dwells within us. David also wasn't able to speak in tongues, which builds us up on our most holy faith (Jude 20). He didn't have anything that we have, yet he encouraged himself in the Lord.

He pulled himself up out of despair and pursued the Amalekites. He recovered everything the Amalekites took from his town, as well as all their spoil. Within forty-eight hours, all of David's dreams had come to pass. He was crowned king and began to fulfill what God had told him to do. But what would've happened if he had just given in and given up? It was critical for him to encourage himself in the Lord.

This is exactly what we have to do. This is what verses 6-8 are talking about. We have to take what Jesus has done for us and sprinkle our conscience, cleanse it, purge it, and get to the point where we can enter boldly into the presence of God. We must encourage ourselves, knowing that God will never leave us or forsake us. And instead of going by how we feel and what our conscience tells us, we need to purge our conscience.

Talk to Yourself

When I first saw in Scripture that I was righteous, I still didn't feel it. I used to live my life just going by what I felt, and I was still transitioning to a life where I based my perspective on the Word of God. I made progress, but I still depended a lot on feelings. I didn't feel that I was righteous, yet I understood that I was because I saw it in the Bible.

In order to help me change how I saw myself, I'd stand in front of a mirror and look at myself eye to eye. I'd point at myself and say, "Andrew, you are the righteousness of God through Christ Jesus." The first time I said that, all the hair on the back of my neck stood up! I thought, *I hope God doesn't strike me dead.* I said to God, "Don't kill me, Lord. I'm just saying what I see in the Bible."

Everything inside of me thought, *This can't be true.* But it's what I saw, and I knew in my heart it was true. I just didn't feel it. I literally stood for hours in front of the mirror telling myself that I was the righteousness of God. I'd also say to myself, "I can enter boldly into the presence of God. God is not angry at me. I have eternal redemption and an eternal inheritance." I continued to quote the Word to myself and preach to myself.

I know some of you think I'm weird, but I think you're weird for allowing yourself to condemn yourself and accepting it, when the truth is that believers have been set free through the blood of the Lord Jesus Christ. It's certainly not God condemning us (Rom. 8:1), and it's not even the devil doing it. We are the ones who condemn ourselves, but we have to encourage ourselves with these truths. You must take the Word of God and cleanse yourself from an evil conscience, and you have to get to a place to where you have no more sin-consciousness.

It's one thing to have me tell you to do this, but it's another to actually do it for yourself. You can get some relief just from having me tell you. But it's your self-talk that's going to establish whether you win or lose. You can read these words and nod your head and say, "Yeah, yeah, I agree with you, Andrew." But what are you saying to yourself? This is what the Bible says. This is what I say. But what do you say?

Do you condemn yourself? Do you beat yourself up over your failures and over your weaknesses? Are you still allowing your conscience to condemn you and make you live a life of unworthiness when the truth is that you have been cleansed? You are the righteousness of God. First John 4:17 tells us that *"as* [Jesus] *is, so are we in this world"* (brackets added). And 1 Corinthians 6:17 says, *"He that is joined unto the Lord is one spirit."* You're one with God!

God's spirit that entered into your born-again spirit is identical to Jesus. All you have to do is purge your conscience and then learn to live and walk in these truths. I promise you that if you could understand and apply what I'm sharing with you, you'd understand why you don't have to have Christian celebrities or others pray for you. You could do it yourself if you knew how much God has forgiven you. If your conscience was purged, you'd see that you have every bit as much access to God as I have. Most people don't understand this.

We Condemn Ourselves

Once, after I taught a message at a church, I was praying for people up front with another minister and his wife. We had a guy come forward who was nearly passing out and hyperventilating. He said to me, "I can't believe I'm talking to you. I get to shake your hand." He just went on and on, and it was way over the top. Finally, I said to him, "You know, if you would spend more time with God, you wouldn't be nearly as impressed with me. The way you're acting shows how little of a relationship you have with God."

That sounds harsh, but it's true. Some people believe that certain people have something more or different when it comes to God than what they have. That is their conscience condemning them. We are the ones who tell ourselves that we are naked. It's our own conscience that makes us feel shameful and inferior. The truth is that, in the spirit, we've been born again. We are as righteous and pure and holy as they come. God's not the one telling us that we have shame. He's not the one pointing out our nakedness. It's us. We condemn ourselves.

These truths that I've been sharing through the Word of God will transform your life if you apply them. But you're going to have to encourage yourself. It's not enough to just have me encourage you. You have to take these things and encourage yourself with them. You must meditate on what I've been sharing. It's taken me fifty years to figure out some of the things that I'm teaching here, but I know that some of you are thinking, *I've heard this before. I got it.* But you need to meditate on it so these principles can get down deep on the inside of you in order for you to benefit from them.

Help Us Enter In

I'd like to close this chapter with a short prayer for you. Be in agreement with me as I pray for you, and trust God to bring these truths to pass in your life:

> *Father, I pray for my brothers and sisters reading this book, and I ask You for wisdom. Help us to enter into the holy of holies by the blood of Jesus, by a new and living way that You have consecrated for us, through Jesus and through His sacrifice. I pray that we would come with full assurance of faith, having our hearts sprinkled from an evil conscience and our bodies washed with pure water.*
>
> *Thank You, Father, for what You've done for every one of us. Help us to acknowledge every good thing within us because of you (Philem. 6). I pray especially for my brothers and sisters who believe in You, who believe that You exist, who believe that You are all-powerful and can do miracles, but don't understand they've been forgiven and still live with sin-consciousness. They are still conscious of all of their failures. They feel unworthy and are unable to receive from You.*
>
> *I pray that the Holy Spirit would reveal these things to us and set us free from all guilt and condemnation. Help us to take advantage of everything that Jesus has purchased for us. Help us to stand boldly in Your presence and to come boldly*

before Your throne of grace, that we might find grace to help in time of need. I pray this for every one of us.

I pray that these truths would be imprinted on our hearts so deeply that we won't ever stray from them. I pray that my brothers and sisters would meditate on these things and that they would look in the mirror and talk to themselves and convince themselves that they are the righteousness of God and that they have been set free. In Jesus's name, Amen!

CHAPTER 16

Assure Your Heart

Hereby perceive we the love of God, because he laid down his life for us: and we ought to lay down our lives for the brethren. But whoso hath this world's good, and seeth his brother have need, and shutteth up his bowels of compassion from him, how dwelleth the love of God in him? My little children, let us not love in word, neither in tongue; but in deed and in truth. And hereby we know that we are of the truth, and shall assure our hearts before him.

1 John 3:16-19

The book of 1 John was written because there were Gnostics in the church at the time of John's writing. The Gnostics thought they possessed a superior knowledge. They were people who said, "We understand more than everyone else. We've got more knowledge than anyone." They took the grace of God and used that

grace to tell people that it was okay to just live like the devil. They taught that a person could commit adultery or anything else and, because of God's grace, it didn't matter.

It's true that regardless of what sin you commit, God still loves you. That's what His grace does. But it's not true that we can live in sin and flaunt our sin and, in essence, thumb our nose at God and then think we'll prosper. These Gnostics would take the grace of God and use it to live in total rebellion toward Him. So, John was saying that they weren't true believers.

His point was that if they were truly born again, they would want to live for God. We've talked about 1 John 3:3, which says, *"Every man that hath this hope in him purifieth himself, even as he is pure."* Those who are born again work to purify themselves. John was saying that you can tell who the true believers are because they have a desire for God. They are seeking to live for God.

No one will live for God perfectly, so you can't say that if you have any failure in your life you aren't a true believer. That's not what John was saying. But he did say that a person who has no desire to live for God has never truly been changed. We have a lot of people in our churches today who do not want to live for God, and they are not truly born again. There are a lot of church members who are going to split hell wide open because their hearts have never been changed. This is what John is writing about and trying to make clear in 1 John.

Looking at verses 16 and 17, we see John showing us one way to determine if we are truly Christians. He said that if you're a believer and your heart has been changed, you will have a desire to be a blessing to people. People who see the needs of others but just ignore those needs make you wonder whether they have the love of God in them. This type of behavior is not consistent with God.

You May Not Know It

Verse 19 says, *"And hereby we know that we are of the truth, and shall assure our hearts before him."* This tells us that this is how we know that we are of God *"and shall assure our hearts before him."* People will read this and completely skip over these words. But what he said here is amazing. You have to assure your heart that you are of God. Do you know that most people don't think that way? Most people think that if they were really right with God, and if God was pleased with them, they would just know it. According to 1 John 3:19, however, we need to assure our hearts before God.

I've talked to hundreds of people who have prayed for salvation, but they don't have any assurance that they're saved. They're just waiting until all doubt, all reservations, and all fear are gone. As long as they feel any fear, and as long as they have any kind of reservations, they don't believe they are truly saved. They assume that if they were saved they would know it. No, that's not how it works. The Bible says that we have to assure our hearts.

The Greek word translated *assure* means "to convince" (*Strong's Concordance*) or to persuade. The exact same Greek word was translated *persuaded* when Paul said, *"For I am persuaded, that neither death, nor life, nor angels, nor principalities, nor powers, nor things present, nor things to come, Nor height, nor depth, nor any other creature, shall be able to separate us from the love of God, which is in Christ Jesus our Lord"* (Rom. 8:38-39). Paul had to persuade himself. He had to assure himself.

Assure denotes a peace of mind about a situation. John was saying that we have to come to a place where we have peace of mind.

The reason I brought this up is to say that our conscience doesn't automatically bear witness and give us confidence. As I mentioned before, it is geared toward condemning us and showing us our failures. Its job is to make us feel unworthy and unaccepted.

First John 3:19 tells us that we must assure, convince, and persuade our hearts that we are of God. You can apply this principle to everything, but a really good example of this is with healing. There are a lot of people who know God can heal. They'll hear a healing testimony and completely agree with it and think it's awesome. They don't doubt at all that it could happen. But then they pray, and they aren't assured. They don't have peace of mind about their healing. They aren't persuaded. They aren't convinced, and they don't do anything to convince themselves. They just figure that if they were healed, all of their doubt would be gone, all of their reservations would be gone, and they would somehow just know it. But that's not so. We have to persuade, convince, and assure our hearts.

Believe and Speak Boldly

As I write this book, I'm in the process of believing God for $180 million for our ministry because I believe this is what God told me to do. He hasn't told everyone to believe for such large sums of money, but He told me to, because that's what it's going to take to fulfill the vision He gave me. I've been speaking what I'm believing for, but I'm just like anyone else. I don't have $180 million. I have to battle thoughts that sometimes tell me I'm an idiot for believing for this much money. At the time of this writing, our ministry needs $7,000 an hour—24 hours a day, 7 days a week, 365 days a year—to survive. Seven thousand dollars an hour! I could easily let that get to me. It could certainly bother me. I have thoughts that come against me like anyone else would, but I assure my heart.

I'll look back at other times that God has delivered me or provided for me. I'll read through scriptures and speak them to myself. I convince myself that God will come through for me. I encourage myself in the Lord, as I taught on in chapter 15. I constantly build myself up, according to Jude 20. I've learned that if you aren't bold enough to say what you really believe and you're afraid of people's reactions, you'll be hindered, and your heart will condemn you. So, I've gotten to the point where I blab my vision out loud. I talk about it all the time. When I talk about my vision, it helps me. When I talk big, it helps me.

I'm telling you this because there are some of you who honestly believe that if God really loved you, you would just know it. No, you wouldn't. You have to assure your heart, and sometimes that means you have to talk to yourself. People come to me all the time, asking me to pray that God would show them His love. They say that they want to feel God's love for them. But I tell them, "No, I won't do it." And they look at me as if to say, "What's wrong with that? That's a good prayer!"

But I tell them, "The Bible says in Romans 5:8, '*God commendeth his love toward us, in that, while we were yet sinners, Christ died for us.'* And John 3:16 tells us that *'God so loved the world, that he gave his only begotten Son, that whosoever believeth in him should not perish, but have everlasting life.'* And Romans 5:5 says, *'The love of God is shed abroad in our hearts by the Holy Ghost.'"* The Bible teaches us that God loves us, and there is nothing we can do about it. You can't make Him love you more, and you can't make Him love you less.

Even if you don't feel His love, you need to just pull your thumb out of your mouth, grow up, and start assuring your heart. Take the Word of God and convince yourself of His love. If you don't feel healed, start praising God anyway that you are healed because His Word says so. Pretty soon, you'll get to where you believe it regardless of how you feel and regardless of the doctor's report. When you get to where you don't care about what anyone or anything else—including your own body—says about it, and you really believe you're healed, then your healing will manifest.

Just Do It!

The process of persuading yourself and assuring your heart doesn't happen automatically. This is where so many Christians miss it, and it all ties in with what I've been teaching throughout this book about the conscience. Your conscience will say, "You're just lying. You're just faking it. You're just acting like you're healed when you aren't." That's how your conscience condemns you. Your conscience will tell you that you're a fool for telling people that God's going to provide you with such a large amount of money so you can fulfill the vision He's given you.

Your conscience will always come against you, and this is why you have to assure your heart. The average Christian does not do this. The average Christian just prays and then takes a passive position. Instead of taking an active position by assuring their heart with God's Word, they take a passive position and pray, "God, make me believe." He's not going to make you believe. He's already put faith on the inside of you (Eph. 2:8). It's up to you to become fully persuaded.

When I teach and minister, I always have people who come to me and ask, "Will you please pray that God would help me to serve Him?" I say, "No. God wants you to serve Him more than you want to serve Him. You don't have to beg and plead and act like it's up to Him whether or not you serve Him. It's up to you. Decide what you want to do, and go do it." Other people ask me to pray that they would get into the Word and renew their mind. I can't pray that you'll get into the Word. Just do it!

I've had people ask me to pray that God would take cigarettes away from them and that they'll quit smoking. What they mean is that they want the desire to smoke to get taken away. They just want it to evaporate all of a sudden so there's no effort on their part. I remind them that when they started smoking, it made them sick. They hated it. They turned green and had to force their body to like it. Well, now they may have to force their body not to like it. Then they say, "But I just can't overcome it."

I ask them, "If I had a gun pointed at your head and told you that if you want to live you can't ever smoke another cigarette, could you quit smoking?" They will say yes. So, I tell them, "See? You can do it. You just lack motivation. You like smoking too much to quit." The average Christian says, "God, I have nothing. I can do nothing. I am nothing. Would You please miraculously do something in my life?" When they say this, they are relinquishing their responsibility and authority.

God has given us authority. He told us to assure our hearts. If you don't feel the love of God, you're wrong. It doesn't matter what you feel like. If you don't feel healed, you're wrong. First Peter 2:24 tells us that *"by* [Jesus's] *stripes ye were healed"* (brackets added). "No," you say, "I'm dying." But I say, "No, you're wrong." You've already been healed, but the problem is that you haven't assured your heart. You aren't fully persuaded. You're going to wait until the pain is gone, until the tumor is gone, until the doctor tells you that you're healed before you really believe that it's done.

Faith, Not Feelings

You may say, "Well, I thought that if God had touched me I'd just know it." But you wouldn't. John 4:24 says that God is a Spirit. He moves in the spirit realm. You're waiting for Him to move in the physical realm so that you can see these things with your eyes. Faith means to believe what you can't see. Hebrews 11:1 says that *"faith is the substance of things hoped for, the evidence of things not seen."* Faith is being able to believe something because God's Word promises it.

If you know what the Word says about your situation, but you can't believe it because you don't feel it, that just means that you are carnal and full of unbelief. When you finally stop glorifying your feelings and looking at your feelings, then you'll have all the feelings you can handle. But when you're making feelings the object of your attention, God will specifically keep you from the feelings because He wants you to *"walk by faith"* like the Bible tells us in 2 Corinthians 5:7. And, in Hebrews 11:6, we learn that *"without faith it is impossible to please him."*

He wants us to be in faith instead of just going by how we feel. I have some wonderful feelings, and I have some great times with the Lord. There are times that I feel God's anointing. I have goose bumps going up and down my spine. I have a lot of things happen that I don't tell other people about because if I did, they'd make a doctrine out of it: "This is how Andrew operates, so unless I feel what he feels, then it must not be working." So, I don't even tell people what I'm feeling.

But the vast majority of the time I don't feel a thing, so I have to go by what the Word of God says, just like I'm teaching here. When you get to where feelings aren't necessary, then you can really feel things. But as long as you make a god of your feelings, God will not help you. He won't reinforce that.

You have to believe that what you're trusting God for is already a spiritual reality. It's a done deal. You need to get to where you rejoice before you can see, taste, hear, smell, and feel it. When you get to where you have convinced your heart that you already have it, then you'll get it. You have to see it on the inside before you see it on the outside. It all starts by convincing and assuring your heart.

In the next chapter, we'll dive deeper into the realm of feelings and find out what's really responsible for making us feel the way we do.

CHAPTER 17

Who Cares How You Feel?

Throughout this book I've used multiple scriptures to establish how our consciences condemn us. Another verse confirming this point is 1 John 3:20:

> *If our heart condemn us, God is greater than our heart, and knoweth all things.*

When John talked about the heart in this verse, he was speaking of the conscience. If you live under condemnation and feel unworthy, shameful, or fearful—and you feel like you aren't worthy to approach God—1 John 3:20 says God is greater than your heart. He knows the truth. In other words, you can feel condemned, you can feel unworthy, you can feel shame, you can feel fear, but God is not the source of it.

This is a huge statement. Most people, especially Christians, assume that if you feel rotten about yourself, it must be God making you feel that way; it must be God who is convicting you. In my teaching *The Positive Ministry of the Holy Spirit,* I talk about John 16:8, where Jesus said, *"When* [the Holy Spirit] *is come, he will reprove the world of sin, and of righteousness, and of judgment"* (brackets added). Religion has interpreted this verse to mean that the Holy Spirit is going to convict you every time you do something wrong. He's going to make you feel miserable. And then He's going to show you that you're unrighteous, and you'll be judged if you don't repent.

God, in His infinite wisdom, knew this scripture would be misinterpreted, so He explained it in the next verse:

> *Of sin, because they believe not on me.*
>
> **John 16:9**

The sin that the Holy Spirit will convict us over is the sin of not believing on Jesus. The Holy Spirit is not going to nail you each time you do something wrong. When you lie, it's not the Holy Spirit who makes you feel terrible until you repent. When you commit adultery, it's not the Holy Spirit who makes you feel rotten and impure.

People attribute these feelings to the Holy Spirit, but verse 8 says that the Holy Spirit reproves the world of sin—singular—not sins. The sin that he reproves the world of is the sin of not believing on Jesus. This is one sin, singular. The sin is that you aren't trusting in Jesus as your Lord and Savior. You aren't believing on Jesus.

Everything the Holy Spirit does for us is actually a positive ministry that draws us back to Jesus. If you're doing drugs, the Holy Spirit won't say, "You sorry thing. Why are you doing drugs? God's really mad at you now." No, the Holy Spirit isn't the one making you feel bad.

The Holy Spirit will, however, tell you, "Why are you turning to drugs instead of turning to Me? I want to be the one who helps you cope. I don't want you to ruin your health and waste your money. Drugs make you lose control, and you could cause a wreck and hurt or kill yourself. I love you. I want to supply your needs." Or, if you're drinking, the Holy Spirit will ask, "Why do you want to turn to the spirits that are in a bottle instead of the Holy Spirit? Let Me be the one to comfort you." With the Holy Spirit, it's not about condemnation; it's about love. He will minister to you in a positive way and not a condemning way.

Continuing in verse 8, John said that the Holy Spirit *"will reprove the world . . . of righteousness."* Not of unrighteousness, but of righteousness. The Holy Spirit won't tell you you're unrighteous because you sinned. Instead, He'll say, "Jesus loves you. You need to allow Jesus to be the one who heals you and helps you instead of turning to something like alcohol or drugs." The Holy Spirit will encourage you that, even though you messed up, you're still righteous. You're still in right standing with God. Your righteousness doesn't fluctuate based on what you did or didn't do.

The third thing that John 16:8 mentions is judgment: *"He* [the Holy Spirit] *will reprove the world . . . of judgment"* (brackets added). John 16:11 tells us that *"the prince of this world is judged."* The Holy Spirit will say to you, "Even though you've sinned, it's still all about you and your relationship with Jesus. He still loves you. Come back to Jesus. You're still righteous. Satan, who's causing you problems by drawing you into sin and condemning you, is the one who has been judged, not you."

Our Worst Enemy

Chances are, you've had someone in your church give a testimony like, "I didn't obey God. I didn't give an offering that He wanted me to give, and the Holy Spirit has made me miserable. He won't leave me alone." Then that person says, "But, I decided I'm finally going to obey God and give the offering." Then everyone claps. You know, that's a sorry testimony, saying that you didn't want to do something, but the Holy Spirit made you miserable until you did. That's not right, and that's not the Holy Spirit.

Your conscience is what made you miserable. It was your conscience that smote you. You knew in your heart that you weren't doing what you were supposed to do, so your conscience condemned you. That's what 1 John 3:20 is saying: *"If our heart condemn us . . . God is greater than our heart, and knoweth all things."* God is not like your conscience. Your conscience will condemn you and make you feel bad and unworthy. It'll make you feel naked before God, just like Adam and Eve. But God is never like that. He is greater than your heart or conscience. He won't condemn you.

I used to think, *God, if You really loved me I wouldn't feel so miserable. I would feel Your love, and I would have so much confidence and boldness that I would just know it. I wouldn't have to work for it. It would just be there.* But these verses showed me that our heart can condemn us. We all have had a conscience that has been totally out of whack. And then religion—the Law—brought it back to a proper standard, made it come alive, and amplified our sin. Those of us who have lived under religion have an overactive conscience that condemns us constantly.

I guarantee you that the average Christian feels unworthy, condemned, and separated from God, when the truth is that God isn't mad at all. It's not God who condemns us; it's our own conscience that condemns us. I don't even believe we can blame the devil. He may have been the one who started it by teaching us the wrong things, but now we're doing a bang-up job of ruining our own lives because we condemn ourselves constantly. The devil can just go on vacation!

I think that sometimes the devil looks at the way we condemn ourselves and takes notes. He thinks, *I never thought of that.* He gets inspiration from the way we beat ourselves up.

We are definitely our own worst enemy. I have people ask me all of the time, "Why is it that I can pray for others and see them healed of all kinds of things, but I can't get healed myself?" There are multiple reasons, but one is because we are more gracious to others than we are to ourselves. We know that other people aren't everything they should be, but we will still minister love and mercy to them, yet we are much harder on ourselves.

The problem is that we know ourselves better than we know anyone else. We know everything we've done wrong, we know about our rotten attitudes, and we know about our negative thoughts. We also know all about our doubts and fears. Because we know ourselves so well, we condemn ourselves. This is why a lot of people can minister love and mercy toward others without having any doubts, but they can't receive it for themselves because they're harder on themselves than anyone else. That's a result of the conscience. God's not the one causing us to feel this way.

First John 3:20 says that our heart condemns us when God isn't condemning us. This totally liberated me when I finally found out that the awareness I had of always being unworthy and unable to do things for God didn't come from God at all. I realized that it was my own conscience. I hadn't purged my conscience with the blood of the Lord Jesus Christ (Heb. 10:2), and I hadn't assured my heart (1 John 3:19). Instead, I was allowing my conscience to function like a spoiled brat. It wasn't being disciplined. It wasn't being controlled. I wasn't dictating to it; *it was dictating to me.*

When I saw that, it changed my life. I quit operating by how I felt and started operating by what the Word of God says. I started letting the Word dominate me. This is so simple you need to have someone help you misunderstand it. Yet people allow their conscience to condemn them, and they continue to feel unworthy. You know, most people don't let the Bible get in the way of what they believe. They say, "But this is how I feel. I don't care what the Bible says."

Who Cares How You Feel?

Years ago, a woman who was a student of ours at Charis Bible College gave me a copy of a message that she had taught. She was really proud of this teaching where she talked about a girl she had ministered to. The girl hated her parents and had completely rebelled against them. The woman also knew this girl's parents, and she said that the parents were good parents—not perfect, but good parents. And the girl had taken offense where none was intended by the parents. The parents wanted her to go to church and had imposed some restrictions on her for her own good, but the girl interpreted their rules as meaning that they hated her. So, the girl took offense and became bitter and angry at her parents.

In her teaching, this woman even said that she knew the girl's opinion was wrong. The girl had taken offense where there was no justification for it. But then the woman went on to say that it didn't matter whether the girl's opinion was accurate or not because, to her, it was accurate. So, as she ministered to the girl, she walked her through the steps of forgiving her parents. When I heard that, I pulled that cassette tape out of my car's tape player and threw it out the window! I was as mad as I could be.

This kind of thinking infuriates me because it is so descriptive of our world today. It no longer matters what's right or wrong. It's all about how people feel. If you feel a certain way, it doesn't matter what reality is. There's an old children's song titled something like "Guess I'll Go Eat Worms." The lyrics are, "Nobody likes me, everybody hates me, guess I'll go eat worms. Long, thin, slimy ones; short, fat, juicy ones; itsy, bitsy, fuzzy wuzzy worms."

Of course, it isn't true that no one likes you and everyone hates you. But you may feel like it is. I call this the Elijah syndrome. Obadiah told Elijah that he had hid one hundred prophets and had been giving them bread and water for three years. Elijah knew there were still one hundred preachers that were serving God (1 Kin.

18:13). Yet in the next chapter when the Lord inquired of Elijah, this was Elijah's response:

> *Behold, the word of the LORD came to him, and he said unto him, What doest thou here, Elijah? And he said, I have been very jealous for the LORD God of hosts: for the children of Israel have forsaken thy covenant, thrown down thine altars, and slain thy prophets with the sword; and I, even I only, am left; and they seek my life, to take it away.*
>
> 1 Kings 19:9-10

In essence, Elijah was saying, "Nobody likes me. Everybody hates me. I guess I'll go eat worms." He knew it wasn't true that he was the only one left. He had facts that said otherwise, but that's how he felt, and that's what dictated his actions.

Then, in verses 11-12, God sent a strong wind, a mighty earthquake, and a fire. In verse 13, God asked Elijah again, "What are you doing here?" You know, if the Lord asks you the same question twice, it's because you answered wrong the first time. If He lets you retake the test, don't give Him the same answer that you did the first time. You'll flunk again.

It wasn't very smart on Elijah's part, but in verse 14, he said the exact same thing as he did in verse 10. After he failed the test the second time, the Lord said to him,

> *Go, return on thy way to the wilderness of Damascus: and when thou comest, anoint Hazael to be king over Syria: And Jehu the son of Nimshi shalt thou anoint to be king over Israel:*

and Elisha the son of Shaphat of Abelmeholah shalt thou anoint to be prophet in thy room.

1 Kings 19:15-16

God told Elijah to go and anoint his successor, and Elijah's ministry was over. A lot of bad things happened to Elijah simply because he operated by his feelings. Acting on feelings instead of the truth cost Elijah his ministry.

Elijah wasn't the only one affected by his actions, however. In 1 Kings 21:13, we see where Ahab killed Naboth because Elijah didn't do what God told him to do. There was also a Samarian woman who actually ate her own son because of the severity of the famine in her land (2 Kin. 6:24-29). The famine came about from the Syrians taking over Samaria due to Elijah not obeying God. People died because Elijah indulged his feelings and disobeyed the Lord.

Grow Up

We need to grow up. Kids don't usually feel like going to school, and they wouldn't go if their parents didn't make them. But part of growing up is when you do things you don't necessarily want to do. You become responsible and do what you have to do, not just what you feel like doing. As a parent, there are times that you don't feel like changing another diaper, but you do it.

We also need to grow up spiritually and realize that, regardless of what we feel like, God loves us. That's what the Bible says. We need to refuse to go by how we feel. If you're believing for healing, you may not look like you're healed, but the Bible says you are. So, in the name of Jesus, you need to act like you're healed. Talk like you're healed. Assure your heart that you're healed. Stand against the doubt and unbelief.

Several years ago, I got a really bad blister on my ear from being out in the sun. After a while, I got tired of it, and I ripped it off. For six years, that spot on my ear never healed! I never went to a doctor about it, but doctors came to me and said, "That's melanoma. You've got cancer. You're going to lose this ear, or worse, you may die."

During this time, I was ministering in Charlotte, North Carolina, and I prayed for two people in one night who at one time had had the exact same thing on their ear, and it caused them to lose part of their ear. They asked me to pray for them, so there I was with this thing on my ear praying for other people's ears. I figured that was a good opportunity to practice Luke 6:38: *"Give, and it shall be given unto you."* So, I'd amplify the healing coming to me by giving it away to somebody else.

For six years, I had people say things to me about my ear and look at my ear. I had to assure my heart by saying, "I don't care what people say, and I don't care what it looks like. I'm standing on the Word of God." I don't know why it took six years to get healed. But it's my fault, not God's. I'm not blaming God at all. I stuck with it and, praise God, the healing finally manifested. Today, I don't even have a scar to show for it. It's completely gone.

More recently, I was driving home one day, just singing and worshiping the Lord. All of a sudden, I started seeing spots everywhere I looked. I guess I had a blood vessel in my eye rupture or something, and it fogged over and I saw spots. Immediately, I started assuring my heart that I was healed. I started speaking to myself. Most of that has since cleared up, but I still have some spots now and then.

I'll look in the mirror and say, "Eyes, I have good news for you: By the stripes of Jesus you were healed. You are healed in the name of Jesus. Blood vessels, you're healed." I talk to them, and my conscience will say, "You're a liar." So, I'll say, "No, in the name Jesus . . . ," and I'll just keep assuring my heart.

I know some of you think that I don't have any problems, and that's the reason I'm strong in faith. But that's not it at all. I have chosen to stand on the Word of God. Any one of you can do this. Any one of you can assure your heart according to 1 John 3:19. You have a choice. Will you believe what you see, taste, hear, smell, and feel? Or will you believe what the Word says?

Often, in my meetings, people ask me to pray for something that they just need to do for themselves, like renew their minds with the Word. Their voice will start cracking when they ask me as they try to make themselves sound pathetic so I'll have pity on them. But it doesn't work for me. "Would you please help me?" they ask. I tell you, the spirit of slap just wants to come all over me. And then they ask, "Why doesn't anything work for me?" I tell them it's because they're not in faith; they're full of unbelief. "But I feel this or that," they'll say. That's unbelief. Who cares how you feel? It doesn't matter how you feel.

You know, unless Jesus comes back during our lifetime, we're all going to die. We sing a song about how when we all get to heaven, what a day that'll be. Then the doctor says you're going there, and you cry. Something's wrong. You need to assure your heart and say, "Jesus, I'm either going to see You really soon, or I'm going to get healed and rub the devil's nose in it."

I'm not afraid of dying. I never really doubted that I'd see my healing manifest, but I knew that if I didn't, I'd go to be with the Lord. This is how you have to look at things. Either way, you're going to win!

CHAPTER 18

It's Up to You

God loves me. He carries my picture in His wallet. He's got an 8 x 10 of me over His mantel. I believe that God is proud of me and pleased with me because of faith, not because my performance is perfect.

I minister an average of over twenty times a week. I finally put a cap on how many times I'll teach, and now I won't minister more than forty times a week. I know you're probably laughing at that, but I'm serious. Not that long ago, I ministered forty times one week and forty-one times the following week. When you talk that much, you're bound to say something stupid. You're going to make a mistake.

There are times that my conscience will smite me about how I shouldn't have said something, and if my conscience doesn't, my wife will do it for me! There are times that I think, *Why did I say that? That was so stupid.* But I just have to assure my heart and remind myself that God knew what a mess I was when He called me. Even so, He is still pleased with me. I don't think God is embarrassed over me. I don't think He's ashamed of me the way that I am about myself sometimes. I have to tell my heart that, despite my flaws, God loves me. It makes me praise God that much more, knowing that He would choose someone like me. If I was God, I wouldn't have chosen me.

At the time of this writing, we have around 650 employees in our ministry, and we look for the cream of the crop to hire. We don't look for people with problems like I have. Yet God "hired" me. It makes me so thankful that God has chosen me. In Numbers 22, there's a story of how God used a donkey to speak to Balaam. It wasn't because that donkey was spiritual or because it had been studying the Word or praying. If God could use a donkey, he could certainly use me.

He could use you too, if you would stop condemning yourself and being so hard on yourself. If you would quit letting your conscience violate you and instead step out in faith, God would confirm His Word through you with miracles (Mark 16:20). Most of us live with a sin-consciousness that prohibits us from being bold and stepping out for the Lord.

No Condemnation in Jesus

There is therefore now no condemnation to them which are in Christ Jesus, who walk not after the flesh, but after the Spirit. For the law of the Spirit of life in Christ Jesus hath made me free from the law of sin and death. For what the law could not do, in that it was weak through the flesh, God sending his own Son in the likeness of sinful flesh, and for sin, condemned sin in the flesh.

Romans 8:1-3

We have to remember that God is not the source of our condemnation. The law of the spirit of life has set us free from reaping what we deserve. It has made us free from the law of sin and death. God has judged Jesus and put our sin upon Him (verse 3). Jesus suffered for us so that we don't have to suffer. This doesn't just refer to suffering in hell, but we also don't have to suffer in this life with an evil conscience. We don't have to suffer with feeling unworthy, separated from God, and unusable. Jesus has set us free from all of that.

Romans 8:4 says, "*That the righteousness of the law might be fulfilled in us, who walk not after the flesh, but after the Spirit.*" The righteousness of the Law makes us as if we've never sinned. We're justified, and our sin isn't imputed to us. We are as pure and holy as if we'd never sinned. You're as holy as you can get! We were created perfectly righteous and holy when we became born again (Eph. 4:24). Someday we will all be just like Jesus in our body and soul. But right now, if you are born again, you are identical to Jesus in your spirit.

These are the truths you need to constantly assure your heart and purge your conscience with. I tell myself all the time, "This is who I am. This is what I have. This is what I can do." And I'll tell you now, this is not something you do one time and it's over. You have to do it regularly. Every time your conscience rises up to condemn you, reassure your heart with God's Word.

If your conscience condemns you a hundred times a day, then fight back a hundred times a day. Some people may say, "I don't want to put that much effort into it." Well then, just go ahead and live condemned. Go ahead and let your conscience keep telling you how naked you are. Go ahead and live in your shame. How's that working for you? I'm telling you there's a better way. Jesus has already done everything. We're blessed. We already have everything we need.

And the good news is, as you start assuring your heart, it gets easier over time. You can train your senses to operate in encouragement instead of condemnation (Heb. 5:14).

If you aren't experiencing God's best, it's not because God hasn't given it to you. It's because you haven't received it, and your conscience and condemnation are your biggest obstacles to receiving from God. I like blaming everything I can on the devil, but the devil isn't the source of most of our problems. Our problems come from our own conscience that condemns us because we're still living under the Law and not New Testament grace.

Your Confidence Has Great Reward

> *If our heart condemn us, God is greater than our heart, and knoweth all things. Beloved, if our heart condemn us not, then have we confidence toward God.*
>
> **1 John 3:20-21**

When we finally reach a place where our conscience isn't condemning us, we will have confidence toward God. Hebrews 10:35 tells us to *"cast not away therefore your confidence, which hath great recompense of reward."* That word *recompense* basically means payback or end result. Our confidence has great recompense of reward.

I taught earlier that an evil conscience can shipwreck our faith (1 Tim. 1:19). Conversely, if our conscience doesn't condemn us, we can have confidence that our faith will reach its desired port every time—the destination we're aiming for. But this is entirely up to us. God won't purge our conscience for us automatically. He's already provided everything we need through His Word to do this ourselves. It's up to us to take the Word of God and *"purge* [our] *conscience from dead works* [so that we can] *serve the living God"* (Heb. 9:14, brackets added).

Use God's Word like a sharp two-edged sword (Heb. 4:12), and resist the devil (James 4:7). Fight against the lies that your conscience tells you and against what you see and hear in the physical realm. Most Christians will not take on this responsibility. They just want God to take away their pain. Their pain has come because they're reaping something that they've sown, or simply because we live in a fallen world.

Satan is always fighting against us, and we can stand and resist or continue to allow our conscience to condemn us. It's not up to God to make our life victorious. It's up to us to take the tools He's given us and use them. The main area where this comes into play is in our personal relationship with God. Many of us don't have confidence with the Lord. We don't have boldness. We haven't persuaded ourselves that God is 100 percent for us. Because of this, we allow Satan to have access to our lives.

Condemnation Has Consequences

When I first became really turned on to the Lord, I was still in a denomination that taught that God was sovereign, and everything that happened was because God did it or allowed it. This denomination believed that God was the one who put sickness on you, God was the one that made your life miserable, and if you got divorced, God caused it. But eventually, I discovered the truth about God and started resisting these teachings, saying that Satan was the one responsible for such things.

Around this time, there was a woman who was like a spiritual mother to me and had always been a big influence in my life. One night she was at my house, along with my wife, my sister, and my mother. We were eating and having a conversation, and the subject of sickness came up. I said that God was not the one who makes us sick. This woman, who was supposed to be more mature and know more than I did, took offense at what I said. She said, "You can't say that. God controls everything."

Rather than just submit to her and let her continue to say this, I said, "No, that's not true." I wasn't angry, but I took a stand for the Word and started speaking Scripture to her. She didn't like it one bit! She dumped on me and began coming against everything I was saying. But I didn't back down. I said, "You're wrong. This is what the Word of God says." I quoted even more scriptures. If I would have submitted to her words, what she spoke would have had an effect on my faith and on what I believed.

Finally, the woman became so upset that she left. When she did, everyone jumped on me like a chicken on a June bug. "How dare you speak to her that way!" they said. "This woman has been your mentor. She's done so much for you." After that, my conscience smote me, and I started thinking, *How could I have done this to her?* I honestly didn't do anything out of anger. I just wanted to stand up for the Word, but it wasn't received well, and I became condemned over it.

It wasn't long before I experienced negative effects from this condemnation. I had put my shield of faith down because my conscience was condemning me, and I felt guilty and vulnerable. My son Joshua was nine or ten months old at the time, and

Satan attacked him with sickness. For three days he didn't eat or even move. He was so sick. When I touched him, he was burning up with a fever. I was praying. I was rebuking. I was fasting. I was doing everything I knew to do. I was saying all the right things, but I wasn't seeing results and became desperate.

Then, my associate pastor, Marshall Townsley, came over to our house. He was sitting on our little stereo cabinet, listening to me complain. I said to him, "Joshua's not moving. Satan's trying to kill my son. What are we going to do?" Marshall unloaded on me and said, "Andrew, you're a hypocrite. You preach God's Word to people, but you don't live it yourself. You're feeling condemned because you think you did something wrong when you stood up to that lady. You're saying the right things, but your heart isn't in it. You aren't persuaded, and you feel like you deserve this because you messed up."

He just kept on, really letting me have it. He told me I wasn't believing God because I felt unworthy, and on and on. What he had said to me was so harsh that, on his way home, his wife rebuked him for treating me that way, and he turned around and came back to apologize. But before he could get back to my house, Joshua was already healed. What Marshall told me was absolutely true. I realized that even though I still believed God could heal, and I was still speaking my faith, I didn't have any confidence.

My conscience had condemned me and shipwrecked my faith. I didn't have confidence that God's power would flow through me because I felt unworthy. I had done something wrong, and it had wrecked my faith. When I saw that, I laid hands on Joshua and commanded the fever off him, and *Boom!* it was gone. Right away he started eating, and he had no more problems.

I can tell you for sure that it was the unworthiness I felt that kept my faith from manifesting God's healing. I believe this happens multiplied millions of times with people. You may be saying all the right things, but do you feel unworthy? Are you being condemned by your conscience? Are you truly assuring your heart and telling yourself that you have right standing with God? You are the righteousness of God because of what Jesus did and not because of anything that you have done (2 Cor. 5:21).

Agree with God

There are many people who have learned the formulas. They go through the motions, but their heart condemns them. And they don't understand how to deal with it properly. I've known a number of people who had believed God for healing, and from the outside, it looked like they were in faith. They said the right things, and everything looked good, but then they died. It made you wonder what was going on.

One such person actually left a diary for people at his memorial service to read. He wrote "I'm tired. I quit. I'm going to go home. I'm ready to go, and I'm not afraid to go." He was seventy years old, and he decided that he wanted to be with the Lord. He knew no one would understand, so he just went through the motions and said all the right things. But in his diary he wrote "I'm through believing. I'm ready to go home."

To everyone around him, it looked like his faith had failed. But he had just stopped believing.

I think some people die because they were living in condemnation and didn't have the assurance and confidence that they needed to be healed. Walking in confidence toward the Lord doesn't happen automatically. What I've shared with you is against the whole flow of this fallen world and even the religious world.

When you talk about having total victory and how God always heals and wants to bless you, get ready to be criticized. I'm criticized a lot because people say, "You're making those who haven't seen their healing feel bad." I'm not criticizing anyone, but I am saying that it's God's will for us to prosper, and there are people who cannot deal with the fact that maybe they've missed something. They would rather blame God than admit it could be their fault because they haven't assured their heart.

If I became sick and died, some people would say, "Andrew always preached on healing and he saw people raised from the dead, yet he died from a disease." That just means that I missed it somewhere. I don't have a problem with that. I've never done anything perfectly in my life. You shouldn't be shocked if someone dies. Satan comes against us all the time, and no one does everything perfectly.

When our soldiers go to battle and get shot, would you treat them like they're a disgrace to our country? Of course not!

They were on the frontlines and got injured or killed in battle. You honor them and give them a hero's welcome. If Satan was to do something to me, instead of thinking, *Well, maybe healing doesn't work,* you should say, "Praise God, Andrew fought a good fight. He just got killed in the process." God has never had anyone perfect, or even qualified, working for Him yet. We all make mistakes. But you can't stay condemned over it.

If nothing else, you'll feel good about yourself, which is a lot better than hating yourself. I'm not talking about your carnal self, but the born-again part of you that God made. You need to recognize what God has done in you and be thrilled with it. God is. He's pleased with who you are. Amos 3:3 says, *"Can two walk together, except they be agreed?"* As long as you're beating yourself up and condemning yourself, you can't walk with God and operate in His power. So, instead of beating yourself up, start praising God for what Jesus has done for you. We've got a lot to praise Him for.

I wrote this whole book to say this: God loves you. I don't care what you've done wrong. I don't care how messed up you are. God still loves you. Don't allow your conscience to remind you that you're naked. If you would tap into the power of the Holy Spirit so you could begin to assure your heart and come to a place where your heart is no longer condemning you, you would be walking in the Spirit. Galatians 5:16 says to *"walk in the Spirit, and ye shall not fulfil the lust of the flesh."*

When you get to this place, you'll see God's blessings manifest in your life. You will start living holier than you ever have before. But you can't get to this place without seeking God and putting Him first. As you do this, I promise that you'll start seeing things begin to work in your life. You will grow in the Lord and manifest His power. There is nothing stopping you but you!

Receive Jesus as Your Savior

Choosing to receive Jesus Christ as your Lord and Savior is the most important decision you'll ever make!

God's Word promises that *"if thou shalt confess with thy mouth the Lord Jesus, and shalt believe in thine heart that God hath raised him from the dead, thou shalt be saved. For with the heart man believeth unto righteousness; and with the mouth confession is made unto salvation"* (Rom. 10:9-10). *"For whosoever shall call upon the name of the Lord shall be saved"* (Rom. 10:13).

By His grace, God has already done everything to provide salvation. Your part is simply to believe and receive.

Pray out loud, "Jesus, I confess that You are my Lord and Savior. I believe in my heart that God raised You from the dead. By faith in Your Word, I receive salvation now. Thank You for saving me!"

The very moment you commit your life to Jesus Christ, the truth of His Word instantly comes to pass in your spirit. Now that you're born again, there's a brand-new you!

Receive the Holy Spirit

As His child, your loving heavenly Father wants to give you the supernatural power you need to live this new life.

> *For every one that asketh receiveth; and he that seeketh findeth; and to him that knocketh it shall be opened. . . . How much more shall your heavenly Father give the Holy Spirit to them that ask him?*
>
> **Luke 11:10 and 13b**

All you have to do is ask, believe, and receive!

Pray, "Father, I recognize my need for Your power to live this new life. Please fill me with Your Holy Spirit. By faith, I receive it right now! Thank You for baptizing me. Holy Spirit, You are welcome in my life!"

Congratulations! Now you're filled with God's supernatural power!

Some syllables from a language you don't recognize will rise up from your heart to your mouth (1 Cor. 14:14). As you speak them out loud by faith, you're releasing God's power from within and building yourself up in your spirit (1 Cor. 14:4). You can do this whenever and wherever you like.

It doesn't really matter whether you felt anything or not when you prayed to receive the Lord and His Spirit. If you believed in your heart that you received, then God's Word promises that you did. "*Therefore I say unto you, What things soever ye desire, when ye pray, believe that ye receive them, and ye shall have them*" (Mark 11:24). God always honors His Word—believe it!

Please contact our Helpline (Phone: (040) 40280718 and let us know that you've prayed to receive Jesus as your Savior or to be filled with the Holy Spirit. We would like to rejoice with you and help you understand more fully what has taken place in your life. We'll send you a free gift that will help you understand and grow in your new relationship with the Lord. Welcome to your new life!

Gospel Truth

with Andrew Wommack

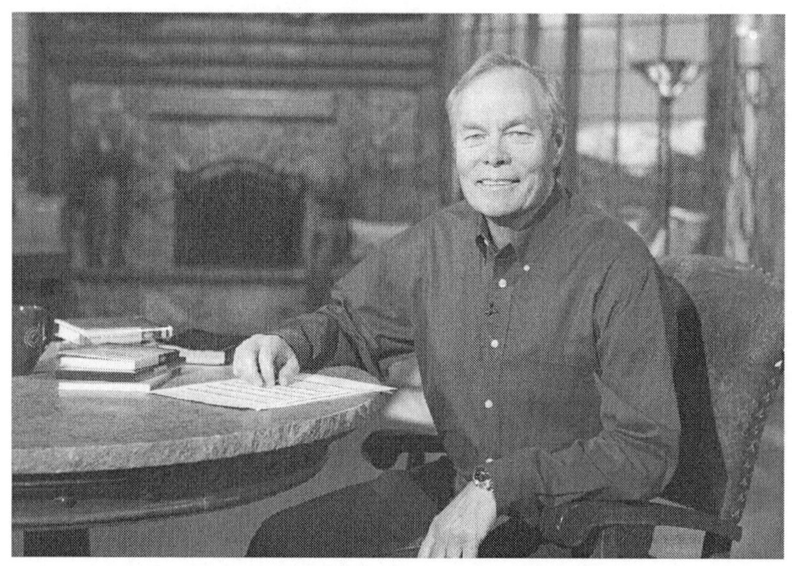

Hearts Transformed

Minds Renewed

Lives Changed

Testimonies come from people all over the world who have immersed themselves in the Word of God.

Watch Andrew Wommack on the daily *Gospel Truth* television program.

For local broadcast times or to watch online, go to **awmi.net/video**.

About the Author

Andrew Wommack's life was forever changed the moment he encountered the supernatural love of God on March 23, 1968. As a renowned Bible teacher and author, Andrew has made it his mission to change the way the world sees God.

Andrew's vision is to go as far and deep with the Gospel as possible. His message goes *far* through the *Gospel Truth* television and radio program, which is available to over half the world's population. The message goes *deep* through discipleship at Charis Bible College, headquartered in Woodland Park, Colorado. Founded in 1994, Charis has campuses across the United States and around the globe.

Andrew also has an extensive library of teaching materials in print, audio, and video—most of which can be downloaded for free from his website: **awmi.net**.

Charis Bible College

Combining the rich teaching of God's Word with practical ministry experience

You have a destiny!
Find it at Charis.

Over 60 campuses across the U.S. and around the world

Convenient distance-education options

Start down the path to your destiny.

Visit **CharisBibleCollegeIndia.org**

to see all our program options, or call (040) 40280718.

Change Your Life.
Change the World.

CONTACT DETAILS

INDIA

www.awmindia.net info@awmindia.net

Locations:

Hyderabad

42-343/1/188, Near Flora Hotel, Maruthi Nagar
A S Rao Nagar, Hyderabad 500 040, INDIA.
Ph: (040)- 40280718

Chennai

72-D, Nandhini Mahal, I Floor, Velachery Main Road
Velachery, Chennai 600 042, INDIA.
Ph: (044)-4202 1820

Mumbai

Bethel, Plot No 305/E, Mith Chowky, Near Girdhar Park
Malad (W), Mumbai 400 064, INDIA.
Ph: +91 8976549515

Delhi

Phone: +91 9560591787

USA

Andrew Wommack Ministries Inc.
PO Box 3333, Colorado Springs CO 80934-3333
www.awmi.net

UK

Andrew Wommack Ministries – Europe
P.O. Box 4392,Walsall, WS1 9AR, ENGLAND
www.awme.net